C A P S T O N E

Smart
THINGS TO KNOW ABOUT...

Your Career

JOHN MIDDLETON

First published 2001 by
Capstone Publishing Ltd (A John Wiley & Sons Co.)
8 Newtec Place
Magdalen Road
Oxford OX4 1RE
United Kingdom
http://www.capstoneideas.com

British Library Cataloguing in Publication Data
A CIP catalogue record for this book is available from the British Library

ISBN 1-84112-114-2

Typeset by
Forewords, 109 Oxford Road, Cowley, Oxford
Printed and bound by
T.J. International Ltd, Padstow, Cornwall

This book is printed on acid-free paper

Contents

What is Smart?

The *Smart* series is a new way of learning. *Smart* books will improve your understanding and performance in some of the critical areas you face to-day like *customers, strategy, change, e-commerce, brands, influencing skills, knowledge management, finance, teamworking, partnerships.*

Smart books summarize accumulated wisdom as well as providing original cutting-edge ideas and tools that will take you out of theory and into action.

The widely respected business guru Chris Argyris points out that even the most intelligent individuals can become ineffective in organizations. Why? Because we are so busy working that we fail to learn about ourselves. We stop reflecting on the changes around us. We get sucked into the patterns of behavior that have produced success for us in the past, not realizing that it may no longer be appropriate for us in the fast-approaching future.

There are three ways the Smart series helps prevent this happening to you:

- by increasing your self-awareness

- by developing your understanding, attitude and behavior

- by giving you the tools to challenge the status quo that exists in your organization.

Smart people need smart organizations. You could spend a third of your career hopping around in search of the Holy Grail, or you could begin to create your own smart organization around you today.

Finally a reminder that books don't change the world, people do. And although the *Smart* series offers you the brightest wisdom from the best practitioners and thinkers, these books throw the responsibility on you to *apply* what you're learning in your work.

Because the truly smart person knows that reading a book is the start of the process and not the end . . .

As Eric Hoffer says, "In times of change, learners inherit the world, while the learned remain beautifully equipped to deal with a world that no longer exists."

David Firth
Smartmaster

Acknowledgements

I'd like to thank . . .

Mark Allin at Capstone, who showed extraordinary levels of editorial patience as I sailed by a number of deadlines for completing this book.

The "Friends of Smart Careers" – an unrivalled group of business brains whose advice, tips, and comments about this book helped me to end up with something that was a vast improvement over my initial attempt. That said, the final decision about what went in was mine, so I alone deserve it on the chin for any howlers, omissions, or glaring errors of judgment. I would try and name everybody but my mind goes back to the 2001 Oscars when actress Julia Roberts gave a gushing acceptance speech, that lasted three minutes over the allotted time. She had managed seemingly to thank just about everybody she knew, only to realize after she sat down that she had left out the real-life Erin Brockovich, the legal secretary whose fight for justice she had brought to the screen. Not wishing to omit anybody, can I simply say to everybody who lent a hand to the content of this book: "Thanks – you know who you are. And if you don't, I'll make sure I tell you next time we're in contact."

All the writers and contributors to *Future Filter*, particularly Bob Gorzynski, Andrew Jones, Ann Rippin and June Burrough, whose regular pearls of wisdom have enhanced my understanding of this post jobs-for-life world of ours.

My parents, George and Dorothy, for their constant love and support and for giving me the space and the confidence to make my own life and career choices. As a parent myself now, I have come to realize just how difficult that is to do.

And finally Julie, and our children Guy and Helena. What can I say to the three of you? You've have borne the brunt of my being husband and father emeritus over much of the past few months. Thank you for helping me to do what I want to do and to be what I want to be. This book is dedicated to you all with love and gratitude.

Preface

Thirty years ago I started work in a world-famous multinational company. By way of encouragement they produced an outline of my future career. "This will be your life," they said, "with titles of likely jobs." The line ended, I remember, with myself as Chief Executive of a particular company in a particular far-off country. I was, at the time, suitably flattered. I left them long before I reached the heights they planned for me, but I already knew that not only did the job they had picked out no longer exist, neither did the company I would have directed, nor even the country in which I was to have operated.

Charles Handy, *The Age of Unreason* (1989)

Q: What's the definition of an archaeologist?
A: Somebody whose career is in ruins.

Career: one's professional life; one's progress in one's job; to rush in an uncontrolled and headlong way

Chambers 21st Century Dictionary

About eighteen months ago, the UK police service announced plans to employ informers on a formal basis, giving them contracts and putting them on the payroll. This was one of the more eye-catching indicators that we now live in a working world increasingly dominated by the knowledge economy. Although we are still in the early stages of this knowledge revolution, we can already see evidence of its impact reflected in ever more volatile markets, and organizes large and small showing increasing uncertainty about future direction.

Linked to this, companies have in recent years become less and less reliant on a large, permanent workforce as they gain more technological savvy and as they try to survive in ever more cost-competitive markets. Michael Dunkerley, in his book *The Jobless Economy*, has put it succinctly: "People are now becoming the most expensive optional component of the productive process and technology is becoming the cheapest."

Against this backdrop, the notion of lifetime employment in one company has all but disappeared. Certainly, at an individual level, many of us are experiencing huge uncertainties about future career and job prospects. If you don't believe me, just ask yourself whether you have a fundamentally different attitude to and expectations of work compared with your parents.

Given that less than half the people of working age in the UK are in full-time permanent roles these days – a drop of around 20% in as many years – it's hardly surprising that "a job for life" seems like a leftover concept from a very different era.

So if the future world of work is destined to become ever more volatile, with a single predictable career line fracturing into a snowstorm of micro-careers, what can we do to give ourselves a better than average chance of survival?

That's where *Smart Things to Know about Your Career* comes in.

This book sets out to give you the resources and information you'll need to thrive in the world of work over the coming years, whether you're intent on making your way inside an organize or whether you want to join – or perhaps already are one of – the growing number of "corporate refuseniks" who pursue self-employment and entrepreneurship, prizing freedom, autonomy and choice above all else.

This book will talk a lot about the practical steps you can take to boost your career prospects and to find the work that suits you best. It will also point you towards sources of information and knowledge about the future that will enable you to make truly informed choices.

Of course, no single book can give you all the answers. This is after all what social philosopher Charles Handy calls the age of unreason, a time "when the future, in so many areas, is to be shaped by us and for us; a time when the only prediction that will hold true is that no predictions will hold true; a time therefore for bold imaginings . . . for thinking the unlikely and doing the unreasonable."

But chances are if you picked up this book then you already recognize that you are the only person with ownership of your career, your skills and the timing of your moves. You are, in short, your own sole proprietor.

For me, this idea was best expressed by Tom Peters, the world's best-known management guru, in an article he wrote for *Fast Company* magazine in August 1997. Titled 'The Brand Called You: You Can't Move Up If You Don't Stand Out', the article is a brilliant synthesis of economic, marketing and business themes that ends with a stark conclusion:

"It's this simple: you are a brand. You are in charge of your brand. There is no single path to success. And there is no one right way to create the brand called You. Except this: Start today. Or else."

So let's get going.

1

A Short History of
Work and Careers

The year is 1901. We're in London.

In your hands, you're holding a copy of the newly published London Post Office directory (the Yellow Pages of its day). As you flick through its pages, you see many of the trades of the day listed. Prominent among them are: ash collectors, blood dryers, ice merchants, lamplighters, livery stable keepers, mourning hatband makers, saddlers, soap makers, soot merchants, spermaceti (whale oil) refiners, and starchers.

Fast forward.

The year is now 2001. We're in Bristol, England. Not that it matters – we're surfing the net so we might as well be anywhere in the world. We go to the website for Electronic Yellow Pages. We use the site's search facility to enter all those trades we noted above from the London Post Office directory. Not one has survived intact. . .

Just look at what's happened to the world of work over the past one hundred years or so: mass production; the rise of 'organization man'; the technological explosion of the 1960s; mainframes; personal computers; the decline of manufacturing; business re-engineering; outsourcing; downshifting; portfolio workers; globalization; the decline of 'organization man' amid a dramatic fall in job tenure; the shortage of knowledge workers; the ascent and descent of the dotcoms; and that's not to mention 101 other phenomena that have shaped organizational thinking and behaviour over the years. To para-phrase Fatboy Slim, "We've come a long way, baby."

The roots of 20th century organizations can be traced back to models of Chinese military hierarchy of a good 2000 years' vintage, and quite probably beyond that too, especially if you extend your search parameters into the natural world. Our concept of "paid work", how-ever, dates back only three hundred years or so to England's Industrial Revolution. Up until that point the world was overwhelmingly rural and the distinction between work and home largely meaningless.

What industrialization was to the 18th and 19th centuries, management was to the 20th. It was Frenchman Henri Fayol who can claim to have defined the core principles governing how organizations worked and the contribution of management to that process. He was the first to sug-gest that management was a discipline in its own right and the first to recognize that the core activities of management were universal, replicating themselves across organizations large and small, across industries, and across national boundaries.

Henri Fayol, 1841–1925

Perhaps more than anybody, Henri Fayol, a mining engineer and manager by profession, defined the nature and working patterns of the 20th century organization. In his book, *General and Industrial Management*, published in 1916, Fayol laid down the following 14 principles of management:

1. Division of work: tasks should be divided up with employees specializing in a limited set of tasks so that expertise is developed and productivity increased.

2. Authority and responsibility: authority is the right to give orders and entails enforcing them with rewards and penalties; authority should be matched with corresponding responsibility.

3. Discipline: is essential for the smooth running of business and is dependent on good leadership, clear and fair arguments, and the judicious application of penalties.

4. Unity of command: for any action whatsoever, an employee should receive orders from one superior only; otherwise authority, discipline, order and stability are threatened.

5. Unity of direction: a group of activities concerned with a single objective should be co-ordinated by a single plan under one head.

6. Subordination of individual interest to general interest: individual or group goals must not he allowed to override those of the business.

7. Remuneration of personnel: may be achieved by various methods but it should be fair, encourage effort, and not lead to overpayment.

8. Centralization: the extent to which orders should be issued only from the top of the organization is a problem which should take into account its characteristics, such as size and the capabilities of the personnel.

9. Scalar chain (line of authority): communications should normally flow up and down the line of authority running from the top to the bottom of the organization, but sideways communication between those of equivalent rank in different departments can be desirable so long as superiors are kept informed.

10. Order: both materials and personnel must always be in their proper place; people must be suited to their posts so there must be careful organization of work and selection of personnel.

11. Equity: personnel must be treated with kindness and justice.

12. Stability of tenure of personnel: rapid turnover of personnel should be avoided because of the time required for the development of expertise.

13. Initiative: all employees should be encouraged to exercise initiative within limits imposed by the requirements of authority and discipline.

14. Esprit de corps: efforts must he made to promote harmony within the organization and prevent dissension and divisiveness.

Fayol also characterized the activities of a commercial organization into six basic elements: technical, commercial, financial, security, accounting and management.

At the same time as Fayol was bringing clarity of definition to the concept of management, Frederick W. Taylor, "the father of scientific management" and arguably the world's first management consultant, was actively taking ideas about how organizations could be most efficiently managed into the workplace.

His work with car-making legend Henry Ford led directly to the mass production techniques that created 15 million Model Ts between 1910 and 1927, and that set the pattern for industrial working practice world-wide. Taylor advocated the use of time-and-motion study as a means of analysing and standardizing work activities. His scientific approach called for detailed observation and measurement of even the most routine work, to find the optimum mode of performance.

Although he lived through little of it – he died in 1915 – Taylor's influence on the 20th century is unquestionable. Peter Drucker, for example, rates him alongside Freud and Darwin as a maker of the modern world. And despite its critics, Taylorism and the production methods that it spawned in the early part of the 20th century, lives on, whether in the form of re-engineering (a direct descendant of scientific management), the continuing debate about the de-skilling of many jobs, or the standardized global practices of companies like McDonald's.

Scientific Management: Taylor's five simple principles

1. Shift all responsibility for the organization of work from the worker to the manager; managers should do all the thinking relating to the planning and design of work, leaving the workers with the task of implementation.

2. Use scientific methods to determine the most efficient way of doing work; assign the worker's task accordingly, specifying the precise way in which the work is to be done.

3. Select the best person to perform the job thus designed.

4. Train the worker to do the work efficiently.

5. Monitor worker performance to ensure that appropriate work procedures are followed and that appropriate results are achieved.

In his biography of Taylor, *The One Best Way* (Little Brown, 1997), Robert Kanigel neatly sums up Taylor's impact on the world of work:

The coming of Taylorism made our age what it was going to become anyway – only more so, more quickly, more irrevocably. Taylor died relatively young. But he lived long enough to take currents of thought drifting through his own time – standards, order, production, regularity, efficiency – and codify them into a system that defines our age.

In its thrall, and under its blessing, we live today.

> Work is of two kinds: first, altering the position of matter at or near the earth's surface relatively to other such matter; second, telling other people to do so. The first is unpleasant and ill paid; the second is pleasant and highly paid.
>
> Bertrand Russell, *In Praise of Idleness* (1935)

Because the industrialists of the early decades of the 20th century followed Henry Ford's lead and put the emphasis on efficiency, it was some years before any significant attention was paid to the needs and motivations of that other major factor involved in the work process – the workers. One of the early pioneers of a view that people were, in fact, central to the world of business was Mary Parker Follett (1868–1933). Although she has achieved an almost legendary status since her death, her views were largely ignored at the time by the business world.

However, the seeds were sown, and a number of people setting up businesses in the 1930s – people like Bill Hewlett and Dave Packard, for instance – began to realize that the nature of the relationship between a company and its workforce impacted explicitly on the quality of contribution that individuals made. Treat people with respect and bear their needs and interests in mind, and they typically make a better contribution. Treat them as production fodder, and they park their brains outside before walking through the gates of the company and into work.

Work in the 20th century – a game of two halves

The workplace of the first half of the 20th century, then, was dominated by efficiency-obsessed Taylorism, and lightened only by a slowly growing realization on the part of some organizations that extracting the optimal performance out of people required a more subtle understanding of the human heart and mind.

Work in the second half of the century also had its dominant themes, the two most significant being:

- The impact of new technology

- The globalization of the economy

The impact of new technology

Technology has become such a part of our lives that we almost cease to notice it. We no longer wonder about how a lightbulb works – a century ago, it would have been amazing.

Similarly, we now take desktop computing for granted, and yet ENIAC, commonly thought of as the first modern computer, was built as recently as 1944.

Since then, the speed of technological advancement has been staggering, particularly in the field of computing technology. ENIAC weighed several tons, consumed 140,000 watts of electricity and could execute up to 5,000 basic arithmetic operations per second. In contrast, PCs these days can weigh less than two pounds, use less than 2 watts of electricity, and execute millions of instructions per second.

If you're a fan of horror movies, you'll know that one particular device used by directors is to play tricks on the audience: lead them into expecting a gruesome shock; build up the tension as the music swells; the door creaks open slowly to reveal . . . nothing. And then, wham, out jumps the bogeyman.

When computers were brought into companies for the first time, predominantly in the 1960s, it was a bit like that. A lot of money was invested over a long period but, fundamentally, nothing changed. There was no significant increase in productivity, and neither were there significant job losses.

And then, wham!

Particularly during the 1980s, it became more and more apparent that the real bottom line of technology was that it made jobs go away. It didn't happen all at once. But, starting in the manufacturing industries and then moving into white-collar work, every day more work was being automated. And both the white-collar workplace and the factory floor were transformed.

As companies gained more technological savvy, they became less tied to time or place, and less reliant on a large, permanent workforce. Against this backdrop, the notion of lifetime employment in one company all but disappeared.

There was of course still work to be done but that work increasingly involved an ability to understand, respond to, manage, and create value from information. However, to unlock the promise of an information economy it became necessary for companies to dismantle the very same managerial hierarchy that once conferred success and order.

Sometimes the future is best viewed from the past. The last big social change in work – the Industrial Revolution – destroyed some ways of life but also made it possible for many people to live far better than ever before. So while agricultural labourers found their jobs disappearing, new and differently skilled jobs sprang up in factories. This phenomenon had a resonance in the late 20th century as people in manufacturing industry found their skills were becoming redundant, displaced by the rise of the service industry sector with its knowledge workers, whose primary talent lies in their ability to develop and manipulate ideas.

What does it all mean?

The impact of information technology on organizations has been significant and can only increase over the coming years. By enabling the creation of a global marketplace, and by decentralising control and empowering people all along the information chain, technology redefines what is possible for organizations. New computer-based systems dissolve conventions of ownership, design, manufacturing, executive style and national identity.

This has profound implications for organizations. Shoshana Zuboff, writing in *Scientific American* (September 1995), argued that technological capability has galloped ahead of our ability to cope, writing that "so far, patterns of morality, sociality, and feeling are evolving much more slowly than technology". To put it another way, our organizational paradigms need to catch up with the new technological paradigm.

SMART QUOTES

Technology, globalization, the shift toward services are breaking down the old social contract, leaving workers at the mercy of a new and ruthless variety of capitalism.

Stan Davis, *Future Perfect*

The globalization of the economy

One of the UK's pre-eminent historians, Eric Hobsbawm, has written extensively about life since the Industrial Revolution. Although the scope of his books goes well beyond work and careers, he provides some brilliant insights into how these themes fit into the broader economic and social picture. So here's Hobsbawm writing in his book *The New Century* (Little Brown, 2000) on the topic of globalization:

> We are certainly a single global economy compared with thirty years ago, but we can say with equal certainty that we'll be even more globalized in 2050, and very much more in 2100. Globalization is not the product of a single action, like switching on a light or starting a car engine. It is a historical process that has undoubtedly speeded up enormously in the last ten years, but it is a permanent, constant transformation. It is not at all clear, therefore, at what stage we can say it has reached its final destination and can be considered complete. This is principally because it essentially involves expanding across a globe that is by its very nature varied geographically, climatically, and historically. This reality imposes certain limitations on the unification of the entire planet. However, we are all agreed that globalization, and especially the globalized economy, has made such spectacular progress that today you couldn't talk of an international division of labor as we did before the seventies.

Of course, globalization and technology are interconnected phenomena. Technology is the enabler of a globalized economy.

In her book *The Death of Distance* (Orion, 1997), Frances Cairncross gave some examples of how this manifests itself:

- *The Death of Distance:* Distance no longer determines the cost of communicating electronically. Companies are increasingly able to organize certain types of work in three shifts according to the world's three main time zones: the Americas, East Asia/Australia and Europe.

- *The Fate of Location:* No longer is location key to most business decisions. Companies can locate any screen-based activity anywhere on earth, wherever they can find the best bargain of skills and productivity. Many developing countries now offer on-line services – monitoring security screens, running help-lines and call centres, writing software, and so forth.

- *More Minnows:* On one hand, the cost of starting new businesses is declining, and so more small companies are springing up to provide services that, in the past, only giants had the scale and scope to provide. Individuals with valuable ideas, initiative, and strong business plans will attract global venture capital and convert their ideas into viable businesses. Small countries will also be more viable.

Economic adolescence is over. The Organization Man worked in a climate warmed by the sun of corporate paternalism. Giant companies such as AT&T ("Ma Bell"), Kodak ("The Great Yellow Father"), and Metropolitan Life ("Mother Met") promised to take care of their workers. But in the late 1980s and early 1990s, when globalization and technology squeezed those companies, as well as the rest of their matriarchal and patriarchal ilk, they booted out their employees like wayward teenagers.

Curiously, dotcom companies revived the family metaphor – only this time Mother and Father were like the cool parents down the block, the ones you always wished were yours. MomAndDad.com gave the kids a huge allowance. They let them have a dog. They turned the office into a rumpus room. And when times toughened? They booted out the kids.

Daniel Pink, writing in *Fast Company*, May 2001

So where are we now?

Life, as we know, is rarely neat. If impact of technology and the globalization of the economy were the two key themes of the latter part of the 20th century, it's clear that these themes are far from being fully played out. They will continue to be the dominant shapers of who does what type of work where.

And where does this leave all of us now, as we try to make build our careers in the early years of the 21st century?

There are some broad conclusions that can be drawn about the state of the working world. Each of the following may carry significant implications for you and your career aspirations:

Traditional jobs still exist – but not here

As Kevin Kelly has put it, "the old economies will continue to operate profitably within the deep cortex of the new economy". The fact is that around the world there are just as many cars and ships being constructed as ever, just as many roads being built, just as much coal being produced, as much steel being made. Eric Hobsbawm writes that it is a mistake to talk of a post-industrial era, because in reality those goods and services that were produced in the industrial era are still being produced today. The difference is where they are now being produced. "Traditional" industries are all thriving elsewhere in the world.

The local labour exchange has become a global job market

Manufacturing capacity will continue to shift from Western economies to those countries with access to cheaper labour. Equally, technology is allowing more and more knowledge-based work to be shipped to the cheapest environment. This may bring jobs to emerging economies but can create severe pressures for unskilled workers in more advanced economies.

Smirk all you like about the Organization Man; his trade-off made possible the 30-year mortgages and college educations that the great American dream was historically made of . . . the old understanding is dead. Interred with it is much of the conventional wisdom on retaining and motivating the American worker.

Staff writer Mary Williams Walsh in the *New York Times*, 6 February 2001

SMART QUOTES

The 21st century knowledge dilemma – to share or to hoard?

According to a study led by Adrian Patch, a research psychologist for Birkbeck College in London, workers have responded to the end of the job-for-life culture by becoming "professional parasites", hoarding their knowledge and expertise. One in five workers thought it was not in his or her interest to share knowledge at work, costing business billions of pounds a year in missed business opportunities, inefficient systems and training.

The study uncovered tensions between companies who have put in computer infrastructures to enable the sharing of knowledge and information, and the willingness of employees to do so. The study found that if companies want to impress a potential permanent employer, they are as likely to share information and seek to build a good reputation as contented staff employees. However, those who feel threatened or unappreciated at work guard their niche knowledge jealously, making effective teamwork virtually impossible. Companies who encourage employees to manage their own careers but who at the same time create dissatisfaction by failing to fulfil their promises risk losing important knowledge that is often a key part of the company's value.

White collars will continue to feel the pinch

Tom Peters predicts that 90% of white-collar jobs in the US will either be destroyed or altered beyond recognition in the next 10–15 years. As he puts it, "That's a catastrophic prediction, given that 90% of us are engaged in white-collar work of one sort or another."

The home as office

As more of us work from home, the line between work and home life will blur. Home design will also change, and the domestic office will become a regular part of the house.

Time to redefine what we mean by a career

We need to broaden the traditional definition of a career. Instead of being viewed narrowly as progression up the hierarchy within an organization, it must now be viewed as the individual's lifelong progression in learning and in work. Learning needs to be continuous and both formal and informal. Work may include not only paid employment and self-employment, but also unpaid work in the community.

The bottom line is that the world of work has changed irrevocably

The collective impact of globalization and technology is that none of us any longer has a career that is a protected species. If there is a cheaper or better quality alternative to you anywhere in the world, you are at risk. Darwin was right: if you can't outpace your environment, you're doomed.

Intel's Andy Grove, puts the challenge for us all bluntly and succinctly in his book *Only the Paranoid Survive* (HarperCollins, 1998):

> Your career is literally your business. You own it as a sole proprietor. You have one employee: yourself. You are in competition with millions of similar businesses: millions of other employees all over the world. You need to accept ownership of your career, your skills and the timing of your moves. It is your responsibility to protect this personal business of yours from harm and to position it to benefit from the changes in the environment. Nobody else can do that for you.

We need, in a nutshell, to be smart about our careers. The rest of this book is designed to help with that aspiration. So let's stop talking about global phenomena and the world of work, and let's start thinking about you.

Interlude 1

The Way We Work

A US survey of 12,000 managers found that those who failed to take a regular holiday in each of the last five years were most likely to suffer from coronary heart disease.

The Guardian, 25 March 2000

A report by *Office Angels* has found that 70% of staff believe that the people they meet outside work judge them instantly by their job titles.

The Guardian, 18 April 2000

A survey by HSBC Bank reports that one in four workers would give up 20% of their pay for an extra day off each week.

Daily Telegraph, 7 April 2000

A report from consultancy International Survey Research has found that British workers are among the most dissatisfied in Europe, followed only by the Italians and Hungarians. The most satisfied are the Swiss, followed by the Dutch, Austrians, Norwegians and Germans.

Financial Times, 18 April 2000

A survey by the Institute of Personnel and Development reveals that 40% of UK workers under 30 think it normal to change jobs every two or three years.

The Times, 13 April 2000

Around 25% of the UK workforce spend some time each year working at home, more than any other country and double the level of 15 years ago.

The Guardian, 29 October 1999

Chris Smith, the government's culture secretary, forecasts that the booming visual media industry in Britain will create 50,000 new jobs.

The Mirror, 4 November 1999

The domestic sector is the fastest-growing service industry in the UK. The £4.6bn we spent on cleaners last year represented a rise of 18.5% over the past decade.

Daily Express, 11 October 1999

Over the past ten years, the proportion of women returning to work after giving birth has risen from a quarter to two thirds.

The Independent, 7 October 1999

Only six years ago, people aged over 50 accounted for 19% of franchisees. Last year, the figure was 29%.

Mail on Sunday, 19 September 1999

An EU survey has revealed that the British work an average of 44.9 hours a week, the longest hours in Europe.

Daily Mail, 15 October 1999

The Old Bailey's 34 court attendants, known as "red armbands", could be facing redundancy. The Home Office is to stop the £950,000 it gives to the Corporation of London which traditionally pays for them.

Daily Telegraph, 25 September 1999

A survey by *Accountancy Age* reveals that out of 600 accountants surveyed, 38% said they wish they had never gone into the profession.

The Mirror, 14 July 1999

According to a new survey 91% of 1,516 business managers questioned said that they worked longer than their contracted hours.

Financial Times, 2 February 2001

A new survey says two thirds of us spend 20 hours a week worrying about work when we should be relaxing.

Daily Express, 26 March 2001

Many senior managers still see themselves as a breed apart. A study of status and perks reveals that:

- In 17% of firms, managers have separate dining facilities

- 38% of managers benefit from health insurance schemes not available to the wider workforce

- 29% have longer holidays than their staff

- 23% have separate toilet and/or shower facilities

- 33% still expect to be addressed as "Sir" or by their title

Survey conducted by the Manufacturing, Science and Finance Union, July 1997

For many of us, work is the place where we can expect to meet our future husband or wife. Yet top companies are banning workplace romances.

Daily Express, 6 October 2000

Ten years ago the average age of the Meridian consultancy's outplacement clients was 45 to 50. Today, it is 31.

Sunday Telegraph, 2 October 2000

Bosses at an Austrian car factory discovered that production was up 8% after painting the toilets bright pink and green. Workers hate the new colour schemes so much that they now spend less time in the loos.

News of the World, 22 March 2001

According to a survey of working mothers by *Mother & Baby* magazine, 81% would stay at home with their small children if they could afford to.

Sunday Times, 9 April 2000

At least 10,000 Japanese die from *karoshi* – death from overwork – each year, according to the National Defence Council for Victims of Karoshi. Surveys of workers calculate the average hours worked at 2,500 hours a year, and as much as 3,000 hours in the banking sector – the equivalent of 12 hours a day, five days a week.

Independent on Sunday, 9 April 2000

A study by *Office Angels* reports that one temp in five is over the age of 45.

The Times, 19 April 2000

One in 10 of the 500,000 business launched each year is headed by people over 50. 71% of businesses started by fifty-somethings are still trading after five years, compared with an average of 50%.

The Guardian, 16 January 2000

Indian restaurants in the UK now employ more people than the steel, coalmining, and shipbuilding industries combined.

The Times, 18 May 2000

Since 1990, the number of barbers in the UK has grown from 18,000 to 70,000. This constitutes the fastest growing employment sector over the past 10 years.

Industrial Society supremo Will Hutton, BBC Television, 8 May 2000

A Mori survey reveals that almost half of Britain's parents still want their children to become lawyers, bankers and accountants, despite the high-profile dotcom explosion and Tony Blair's attempts to turn Britain into a nation of entrepreneurs.

Mail on Sunday, 7 May 2000

Company drivers clock up an annual total of estimated 8.2 billion unnecessary business miles with the sole purpose of minimising their tax liability.

The Guardian, 17 January 1998

2

Taking Stock

In this section, you are encouraged to take a look at your career to date.

Some of you will have progressed to where you are now in a smooth and trouble-free manner; others will have had a more problematic passage. Whichever applies to you, I would heartily suggest spending time on some or all of the exercises in this part.

"So what do you do then?"

Let's face it – it's a question we've all asked or been asked. We meet somebody for the first time – say at a party or a wedding – and one of the first ways we try to pin down the person we're talking with is to find out what they do for a living. In these more egalitarian times, we're not necessarily that bothered about whether we're stood opposite a captain of industry or a plumber – we just want to know. (Come to think of it, if you meet a halfway plausible plumber, make a note of their telephone number – they're like gold dust where I live.)

The point I'm trying to make is that the work we all do continues to define a large part of how we view others and how we regard ourselves. For many of us, our work is inextricably bound up with our self-esteem and our view of how the world is and what life holds for us.

If the work we do is such a central part of our lives, it's seems remarkable that so few of us seem to actively manage our careers. According to a survey reported in the *Daily Mail* (31 January 2000), 64% of all UK workers believe they are in the wrong jobs, with the most dissatisfied people working in accountancy, healthcare, insurance, the motor trade and retailing.

I think most of us are looking for a calling, not a job. Most of us, like the assembly line worker, have jobs that are too small for our spirit. Jobs are not big enough for people.

Nora Watson, from the book *Working* by Studs Terkel

So why are around two-thirds of the UK's working population prepared day after day to go into a job that they seem to dislike so much?

- For the money? That's the simple answer. Few of us have sufficient financial independence to be able to choose not to work.

- For the social contact? Probably. Ask anybody who has left a company what they miss most and the people they worked with will normally come pretty near the top of the list.

- For a sense of security? For some of us, a regular income and a familiar place at which to work help to make life more predictable, more manageable. What an illusion! It's a curious piece of psychology that having a salary coming in at the end of this month convinces us that it's OK to book next summer's holiday, particularly as there have been around five million redundancies in the UK over the past five years, and most surveys show that workers, notably males with long tenure, are more frightened than ever of losing their jobs.

- Because of a lack of alternative? "Let's hang on," sang the Four Seasons some years ago, "to what we've got." Underpinning many people's thinking about their careers is a bird-in-the-hand mentality. Knowing that there are no more 'jobs for life' can leave us clinging all the tighter to what we already have, even if we would rather be doing something else. We try to convince ourselves that it would be madness to chuck in a well-established career path. "I'm a senior manager on a good salary," one of my clients told me once, "How can I justify giving that up to go off on a whim and set myself up as a furniture restorer?"

"I don't know how we got here but, now we're here, let's stay a bit"

Many people would like their lives to have some predictability. The old model of a career, in which people worked their way up the ladder at a single company, delivered the stability that some workers thought was their birthright.

But in a world of flattening hierarchies, collapsing industries, intensifying competition and revolutionizing technology, sometimes the only

options available seem to be either staying at the same level, insecure and deeply frustrated, or joining the ranks of the downsized.

There's another problem. Staying where you are might be acceptable if "where you are" is where you intended to be. All too often, though, where we find ourselves in the working world is not a reflection of positive career intent, but a reflection of career drift.

The accidental career

I spend quite a bit of my time coaching and mentoring people of varying levels of seniority inside organizations. I also work with people who are in what is euphemistically called career transition. You know who I mean: the outplaced, the downsized, in short, the redundant.

Anyway, one theme that occurs time and time again in our conversations is that so many of us just fall into the work we do through chance circumstances rather than positive choice.

I met a man at a charity do a little while back. He was an optician. His father had been an optician. His son had just finished training . . . as an optician. Now optometry is a fine and noble profession and I have a high regard for people working in that field. But it's a bit of a coincidence don't you think.

And permit me to enter the career confessional for a moment. I too have had an accidental career. After I left college, I bummed around for a bit before moving to London from Somerset to set up house and form a band with three old schoolmates. Being strapped for cash until the anticipated performance and royalty cheques turned up, I took a temporary job as an accounts clerk with the then British Airports Authority.

Twelve months later, the band folded. Twelve years later, I was Training and Development Manager at Gatwick Airport. In the intervening time, I had drifted into a permanent accounts job, and then took an internal transfer into personnel (driven more by horror at the thought of taking accountancy exams than anything). I was "encouraged" to pursue a professional qualification to consolidate my personnel career. The rewards looked good and personnel looked like a reasonably comfortable area to stay in. Once I was qualified, it seemed perverse to do anything else. I got locked into earning a decent salary that I couldn't match anywhere else given that I would have dropped to the bottom rung of a new career structure.

Eighteen years after the band fell apart, I was a heartily disillusioned HR professional. Somewhere along the line, I had forgotten to ask myself what I really wanted to do.

It's only after you arrive at a destination that you were never headed for that it becomes apparent you have an accidental career. I'll bet that goal

Try to be the second- or later-born

This is not something that you can do much about at this point of your life, but you might be interested to learn that birth order may play a part in determining the type of career you are well suited to. Research suggests that while first-borns make good, do-it-by-the-book managers, the later-borns are more likely to be mavericks. Both Bill Gates and Rupert Murdoch are second-borns.

Smart things to say about your career

setters achieve twice as much as those who just bumble along without any goals. Not making a choice is a choice in itself.

Managing your career with intent

Chances are that you already have a more coherent view of what you want to be than I did during my personnel phase. If, on the other hand, your career has drifted and meandered to its current resting-place, take heart. It is never too late to confront your career demons.

By collecting data about yourself and your past successes, your skills, your work values, your personality profile and your preferred behaviour patterns, you can quickly have a sound basis for determining how suited you are to the role you are currently filling and from that point explore where you and your career should be heading.

What follows then are several exercises and ideas designed to help you conduct a career stock-take.

SMART QUOTES

In the industrial age, information was like gold. In the digital age, it is like milk – use it quickly.

Consultancy NUA's advertising slogan, quoted in *Information Strategy*, September 1998

Although there's nothing to prevent you from skipping these exercises, I would encourage you to devote some time to them. Completing them may help you gain a new understanding of your personal career issues or may simply reinforce the understanding you already have. Either way, this self-knowledge is the basis of any future action plan.

Smart things to say about your career

A survey in 1999 by the travel company Thomson claims that one person in four seriously considers quitting their job while relaxing on holiday. There's no doubt that giving ourselves a bit of space and time to mull things over can yield some helpful insights.

Here are four smart ways to free your mind:

1. Journalling: Buy a notebook and, every morning as soon as you get up, write three pages of anything – problems you encountered the day before, ideas, dreams, rambling thoughts. Set aside 30 minutes every morning for writing.

2. Sources of surprise: Try to give your mind a new experience every day. Listen to different radio stations, buy a different magazine or newspaper, go into work by a different route. And remember that travel is the best single way to immerse yourself in unfamiliarity; amongst other things, it forces you to ask questions about why people live the way they do and what they value.

3. Network: Share ideas with colleagues. Make a point of seeking the views of others

4. Relax: Listen to music, take a walk, go for a swim – anything that will give you time to unwind and let your subconscious do its work.

Exercise 1: your story so far

Starting as far back as you like and coming up to the present day, identify and make a note of the key events in your life. These might include your education (courses undertaken, exams passed, etc.), family and relationships (parents and siblings, growing up, leaving home, births/deaths of significant people in your life, etc.), personal achievements, and work (jobs, promotions, disappointments, etc.)

Put these into the sequence in which they happened and then, using a decent-sized sheet of paper, plot these key events onto a line you draw to represent your life to date. Pay particular attention to where the peaks and troughs occur. The line might be straight, might look like a rollercoaster, or could be something else entirely – you choose.

When you've finished this, ask yourself any of the following list of questions that seem relevant:

- What have been the highs of your life to date? What made them highs? And the lows? Are there any common themes in either the highs or lows?

- In which elements of your career have been most successful? And least successful?

- What aspects of your career to date have you enjoyed the most? And the least?

- More specifically, which has been the most satisfying role you have undertaken in your date?

- With the benefit of 20:20 hindsight, are there any points in your career or life where you would have made a different choice or decision?

- Has anything surprised you about what has emerged from this exercise?

- What overall conclusions do you draw from this exercise?

Edgar Schein

Different people look for different things out of their careers. Some people look mainly for a sense of security and stability, while others seek out roles with a high level of challenge. Some want to manage people and resources; others prefer to pursue roles requiring a high level of technical competence.

Edgar Schein, Professor of Management at the Sloan School of Management, Massachusetts Institute of Technology, and widely acclaimed as one of the founders of the field of organizational psychology, has suggested that each of us has a particular orientation towards our work, and that we all approach our work with a certain set of priority and values.

To help us articulate these, Schein offers the concept of "career anchors". A career anchor, says Schein "is a combination of perceived areas of competence, motives, and values that you would not give up; it represents your real self", He claims that most people see themselves in terms of the following eight categories of career anchor:

1. *Technical and Functional Competence:* People with this competence have a talent for a particular type of work, and it is the technical content of their work that they wish to specialize in. They have a strong drive to develop their expertise in their specific field.

2. *General Managerial Competence:* For these people, it is management *per se* that interests them. They would view specialization as a trap to be avoided, preferring to seek out high levels of responsibility, varied and challenging assignments, and leadership opportunities.

3. *Autonomy and Independence:* These people have at all times an over-riding need to do things their way, in their own time, and to their own standards. They don't like being bound by other people's rules, procedures, working hours, dress codes, etc. They find organizational life restrictive, irrational and intrusive.

4. *Security and Stability:* These people seek out jobs in apparently strong and reliable organizations that seem to offer job security, have a reputation for avoiding layoffs, and that offer good pension plans. A concern for security and stability guides and constrains all major career decisions throughout an individual's working life.

5. *Entrepreneurial Creativity:* These people are absolutely committed to creating new organizations, products or services. They are restless by nature and constantly require new creative challenges.

6. *Service and Dedication to a Cause:* These people enter certain occupations because of core values that they want to embody in their work. There is an underpinning desire to want to improve the world in some way. Although some occupations might seem to lend themselves to those with a service orientation, the important thing is the attitude of the individual. Doctors, for example, may appear to be anchored here; in reality they are just as likely to be anchored in technical/functional competence, or autonomy, or security.

7. *Pure Challenge:* Some people define success as overcoming seemingly impossible obstacles, solving unsolvable problems and winning out over tough competition. These people don't mind where they find the challenge but it has to be there. Without opportunities to constantly test themselves, they become bored and irritable.

8. *Lifestyle:* For these people, integrating personal life, family life and careers is the most important aspect of their career. They seek flexibility and are unwilling to make sacrifice their life balance for their job. For example, they often sacrifice career advancement rather than relocate.

Can a person have more than one anchor?

According to Schein, there is room for only one career anchor at the top of a person's hierarchy. This anchor represents the one thing a person would not give up if forced to make a choice. Because career roles can allow many anchors to be satisfied – a training manager in a paternalistic company, for example, could simultaneously be fulfilling technical/functional, managerial, autonomy, security and even lifestyle anchors – it is quite possible that an individual never explicitly identifies their one over-riding anchor. However, when the anchor goes missing from the mix – for example, when a technically/functionally anchored person gains promotion to a general management role and has no opportunity to satisfy their core anchor – people can still perform competently but they will probably feel that the real them is not being engaged.

More information on career anchors can be found in Edgar Schein's *Career Anchors: Discovering Your Real Values* (Jossey-Bass Pfeiffer, 1990). This booklet contains a Careers Orientation Inventory that would enable you to establish your dominant anchor (if it's not already apparent to you from the abbreviated descriptions above).

Exercise 2: what do you want from work?

Ah, there's nothing more exciting than science. You get all the fun of: sitting still, being quiet, writing down numbers, paying attention. Science has it all.

Principal Seymour Skinner, from *The Simpsons*

An important part of your self-analysis should include what it is you hope to achieve from working. Are you looking for money, status, a comfortable working environment, to feel part of team, to do something socially worthwhile? And before you answer "Yes" to all of the above, reflect on the extent to which your goals are compatible with each other. High pay for low hours and low stress may be attainable but it's not going to be easy.

You may find it helpful to note what your objectives are under the following headings:

- **Money:** As much as possible? Enough to live on? Not important any more?

- **Working hours:** How many would you like to work? Nine-to-five or non-standard? How much holiday? How much flexibility would you like?

- **Risks:** Do you like to gamble, or is only a very low level of risk in your career choices acceptable? Would you take calculated risks?

- **Stress:** Are you looking for lower levels of stress? Can you cope with stress? Are you aware ever of being under stress at work?

- **Type of work:** Do you want to be able to do the work you like? Do you want to concentrate on what you are good at? Are these two the same? Are your skills being utilized or wasted?

- **Independence:** Are you happy being told what to do? Would you be happy working on your own? Do you think you can do better than your boss?

- **Achievement:** Do you like having big challenges to overcome? Are you attracted by the idea of building a successful business of your own? Do you set yourself high standards to achieve?

- **Power:** Do you prefer to lead rather than be led? Is status important to you?

- **Technical competence:** Does the idea of being regarded as an expert appeal to you?

- **Life balance:** How important is it for you to balance your personal, family and career requirements? What is your ideal balance between these three?

- **Location:** How flexible are you about where you work?

Only 31% of Londoners can get to work in less than 20 minutes compared with 62% of people in the rest of the UK.

Observer, 6 February 2000

There was a survey quite recently about what people most wanted at work. Here's the top ten:

Smart things to say about your career

1.   Being able to work fewer hours
2.   A change in the company culture
3.   Work flexible hours
4.   Reduce commuting – or avoid it
5.   Work from home
6.   Change jobs or relocate
7.   More staff
8.   Earn more
9.   Retire
10. Reduce stress

The top five sacrifices people make for work

1.   Missing the children growing up
2.   Work put before home and family
3.   Moving home for employer
4.   Missed leisure/hobby time
5.   Being away from home short-term

Exercise 3: where am I?

Here are 20 questions to consider. Again, go for the ones that most interest you:

1. How are you feeling about your career right now? Moving along nicely? Stalled? Going well but not happy?

2. How's your self-esteem?

3. How do you feel when you get up to go to work in the morning?

4. What aspects of your current job do you enjoy the most?

5. What aspects of your current job do you enjoy the least?

6. Are you thriving or just hanging in there?

7. When did you last enjoy yourself at work?

8. Do you enjoy working with others?

9. Does your reputation work for or against you?

10. How are you regarded by the people you work with? What would they say about you?

11. Do subordinates, peers, and senior managers hold different views about you, and if so what conclusions can you draw from this?

12. Do you have customers and how do you get on with them?

13. Do you get good interesting assignments to undertake?

14. Is there room for professional and personal growth (a) in your current role? and (b) in your current company?

15. Does you boss support your career development? Is there any gap between the rhetoric and the reality?

16. Do you get stuck on low-profile projects of debatable value?

17. Do you feel that you "fit" with the organizational values of the companies you have worked for. If you don't, what are the points of difference?

18. Have you had a new boss recently, say in the last two years? What impact did this have?

19. How ambitious are you these days?

20. What do you want out of the work you do? Are you getting it?

SMART VOICES

Below are 10 questions that Thomas Stewart has designed as a career wake-up call. If a number of these click, you need to act:

1. Have you learned anything new in the last six months?
2. Is your job easy?
3. Could somebody do your job for less?
4. If your job were open, would you get it?
5. Are you being milked by being kept in the same role? If the answer is yes, where will that leave you in a couple of years time?
6. Do you know what you contribute?
7. What specific skills could you take to the market place right now?
8. What would you do if your job disappeared tomorrow? Next year?
9. Is your heart in the work you're now doing?
10. Are you worried about keeping your job? (If you are, you probably should be.)

Taken from Thomas Stewart, *Intellectual Capital* (Nicholas Brealey, 1998).

Exercise 4: do you like where you work?

Try doing one or both of the following:

Characterizing the organization – in pictures

KILLER QUESTION

Do you respect your current employer?

Draw a picture that symbolizes your view of the place where you work today. (If you struggle to come up with an idea, try imagining that the organization is a vehicle of some sort. Would it be, for example, a sleek Ferrari, an old jalopy, or something else entirely?)

Characterizing the organization – in words

Write a short story that for you sums up your current organization in a nutshell.

How do you assess what you have come up with?

Exercise 5: constraints

It's all very well deciding that all your career needs to go stratospheric is to take time out to go off and do a full-time MBA at Harvard. In reality, for most of us, there are constraints on what is possible in career terms. Some of these constraints may be substantial long-term limitations, and others may only be short-term. Some may be illusory – as Richard Bach, author of *Jonathan Livingston Seagull* once wrote, "Argue for your limitations and, sure enough, they're yours."

Try listing the constraints affecting your career choices over the next few years. They may include financial issues, qualifications, where you live and work, your ability to relocate and so on. After each constraint, make a brief note of the status of that constraint.

For example:

- *Constraint:* Youngest child taking A levels next year – don't wish to disrupt her preparation by moving elsewhere.

- *Status:* Short-term limitation only, although with family and friends in this area I would prefer to avoid moving if at all possible.

Exercise 6: talent show

So what are you good at? All of us have a number of talents. Some of them we are able to use at work; others only come out when we're not at work, or are not drawn on at all. Sometimes our greatest skills are employed outside the context of paid work.

Here is a short list of talents

organizing	giving feedback	completing what you start
motivating people	performing	working with numbers
teaching	writing	being persuasive
leading	growing things	athletic
inspiring	exploring	strategizing
designing things	negotiating	music
building things	planning	being assertive
being loyal	co-ordinating	being discreet
listening	being decisive	mending things

Currently, which of these talents do you have? Are you able to deploy them in your work? Would you like to deploy them in your work? Can you think of other talents that apply to you? Are there talents – either listed above or others that you can think of – that you would like to develop?

Exercise 7: recognizing our achievements

We often don't give ourselves credit for the skills and abilities we have, instead taking them for granted. Can you write down 30 or so achievements you have made in your life that you are really proud of? Alongside each achievement, make a note at the underlying skills or abilities you drew on in order to succeed. If listing 30 achievements sounds excessive, please persevere. There's a tendency for people to do this exercise on automatic pilot to begin with. By the time you're up to achievement 23, you'll start surprising yourself at all you have done that has slipped from immediate recollection.

Smart things to say about your career

Build a personal stock-take into your schedule, say every six months. Ask yourself how happy you are with your work, your health, your social life, and your relationships. Are you happy to re-commit yourself in all these areas or do you want to make changes?

Exercise 8: planning for the future – the best of times, the worst of times

1. Make a list of the five worst things that could happen to your company and your career and develop a strategy for positively tackling each one.

2. Now make a list of five things you would like to make happen to your career. Again, come up a strategy for tackling each item on your list.

KILLER QUESTIONS

What do you want out of your career? Financial rewards? Security? Variety? Intellectual challenge? Adventure? Competitive environment? Something else? What trade-offs are you prepared to make?

Warren Bennis

Warren Bennis is an American business writer, management consultant and former university president. His books include *Co-Leaders* (1999), *Organizing Genius* (1997) and *Leaders: The Strategies for Taking Charge* (1985), which he co-authored with Bert Nanus.

Here's Bennis on success:

> I used to think I wanted to be a university president. And for seven godforsaken years I did just that. The problem was that I wanted to *be* a university president, but I didn't want to *do* a university president. In retrospect, I realized there was an unbridgeable chasm between my aspirations and what actually gave me satisfaction and happiness.

> Based on that experience, I developed a four-question test aimed at anyone seeking "success." You have to answer with complete honesty, which means you have to have a fair amount of self-knowledge.

> 1. Do you know the difference between what you want and what you're good at?

> 2. Do you know what drives you and what gives you satisfaction? (Clearly in my own case, I didn't.)

*SMART
PEOPLE
TO HAVE
ON YOUR
SIDE*

3. Do you know what your values and priorities are, what your organization's values and priorities are, and can you identify the differences between the two?

4. Having measured the differences between what you want and what you're able to do, between what drives you and what satisfies you, and between your values and those of your organization – are you able to overcome those differences?

If you are, then success will be yours. In a nutshell, the key to success is identifying unique modules of talent within you and then finding the right arena in which to use them.

Warren Bennis, quoted in American business magazine Fast Company, June/July 1997.

SMART QUOTES

However brilliant your skills, if they make you a bore, unable to converse with those outside your speciality, if your work does not deserve to be loved because it damages other people, if you are so busy with detail that you've no time to acquire wisdom or exercise your imagination or humour, then no amount of status or financial reward will compensate you for your inadequacy as a human being.

Oxford historian Theodore Zeldin, quoted in People Management, 28 October 1999

. . . and relax

If you've gone through all, or even a few, of these exercises, then by now you will have a lot to mull over. It would be presumptuous of me to try and second-guess what conclusions you are drawing about the current state of your career and related matters. If you believe that everything is fine and dandy for now, then I'm delighted for you. If, on the other hand, you want to look at making some changes in the future, here are some options you might like to consider:

Re-balancing your life

- Change the way you divide income generating and caring roles within your family.

- Spend more time with your family and/or friends.

- Spend more time on leisure activities, hobbies or personal relationships.

- Divide your time between a number of different income generating activities (often called a "portfolio career" – more of this later).

- Devote more time to the local community, church or voluntary activities.

- Become involved in environmental and/or political matters.

- Increase the variety of activities you undertake.

Re-skilling or reinventing your career

- Undertake part- or full-time education to improve your chances in the job market or in launching a new career.

- Improve technical skills to provide you with better job prospects or give you a more rounded experience base.

- Work in a medium or small sized business environment rather than a corporate one.

- Move to a different (i.e. more interesting and ideally growing) industry sector.

- Improve long-term remuneration by moving from the public sector or traditional economic sectors (automotive, banking, retailing, etc.) to new dynamic sectors of the economy (high technology, information, media, etc.).

Downshifting

- Deliberately decide to sacrifice part of your income for a better quality of life.

- Relocate from expensive urban areas to cheaper rural or mixed urban/rural areas.

- Reduce financial commitments in those areas not firmly aligned to core values and security.

- Move from a full-time to a part-time work arrangement (and re-balance as above).

- Make your work a source of enjoyment by aligning personal interests with working activities.

Enriching your life in other ways

- Gain independence through self-employment.

- Eliminate commuting time by working (partly or wholly) from home.

- Make a business from something you love (a passion or an interest) or something that you believe that you were born to do (a mission).

- Leverage skills and abilities that have been under-utilized in your career to date.

- Realign yourself to be true to your deeper values and beliefs.

- Move location within your own country or try living in another country.

KILLER QUESTION

Now that you've spent some time reviewing your career to date, what are you going to do about it?

3

Attributes of a Smart Careerist

No matter what career route is followed – whether that of an entrepreneur, a consultant or a corporate career-maker – there are a number of attributes that the Smart Careerist should either have or will need to work to develop.

The good news is that they are all achievable through practice

The bad news is that there are fifteen of them

The really bad news is that there are actually more than fifteen. (Nobody said this was going to be easy.)

Broadly speaking, competencies are the skills or characteristic actions used by individuals to enable them to cope successfully with a variety of situations both within and outside of work. Competencies, in a nutshell, define the skills and behaviours that are directly related to superior performance in a given role.

According to research conducted a little while back by Roffey Park, over 70% of UK organizations now have competency systems in place. These systems cover anything from the key roles in a business through to some companies where literally every job has its own set of defined competencies.

As well as most organizations, most professions have also created their own set of standards using competency frameworks.

And not just the obvious professions like personnel, accountancy etc. In 1999, for example, The British Standards Institution published a professional standard for nightclub bouncers. The core requirements for bouncers, in case you're interested, are diplomacy and courtesy, moderate language and decent personal appearance, plus an awareness of controlled drugs, an ability to read body language and first aid training.

The competencies required for effectiveness in a given role are often signaled when a job is advertised. In the early part of 2001, New Zealand's spy agency, the Secret Intelligence Service, placed several advertisements in the press in an attempt to recruit secret agents. According to the ad, the job requires "people who have excellent communication and interpersonal skills, flexibility, good judgment, initiative, strong analytical skills and the ability to work in and lead teams".

Although the headings change from company to company and from profession to profession, the following are some of the most commonly found elements of a competency model:

Achievement drive	Judgement
Analytical thinking	Leadership
Business integrity	Networking
Business knowledge	Openness to ideas
Change orientation	People development
Communicating and influencing	Planning and organization
Contribution to results	Preference for action
Creative thinking	Problem solving
Customer focus	Professionalism
Decision making	Self-confidence
Facilitation	Strategic thinking
Financial management	Teamwork
Handling information	Technical knowledge
Innovation	Tenacity
Interpersonal sensitivity	Thinking skills

In order to be effective in a given role, the Smart Careerist could need to have an above average capability in any combination of the 30 competencies mentioned above.

However, the observation that we need to be good at what we do in order to get on doesn't really take us very far. Many of us are highly effective in the roles we perform. Far fewer of us can claim to be brilliant managers of our own careers. We can all too easily get bound up in the day-to-day business of "doing our job" – all too rarely do we make the time needed to construct and manage our careers.

Part of the problem is that we don't normally get any feedback about how well or badly we are managing our careers. Think about the last appraisal you had (assuming it wasn't cancelled or postponed by your boss). Lots of "you did this part of your job brilliantly/well/terribly/not at all", I daresay; perhaps some time spent on how well you demonstrate the competencies most relevant to effective performance of your role, and maybe a bit of time spent on your development needs over the next twelve months (so that you can do your current job even better). But I doubt very much if your boss said anything like: "I'm concerned that you're not spending enough time planning your next job move. You should be networking more. And when was the last time you updated your CV?"

No, the general assumption is all too often that performing well in a given job is all that matters; look after your job and somehow your career will take care of itself.

Generally speaking, then, we get little encouragement from any third parties to devote time to managing our careers. It's ironic that for many people the first time that a company makes an active investment in their career development is paying for outplacement support when they are made redundant! And even then, there is arguably more guilt than altruism behind the company's offer of outplacement.

And we are often just as culpable ourselves, falling into the trap of concentrating on the here and now at the expense of planning for the future.

On the bright side, the fact that you're reading this and maybe other books on making the most of your career suggests that you would prefer your career to unfold with intent rather than by accident.

We all want to have a Smart Career, and we know that there's a lot more to career management than a wash and brush up for your CV and lingering over the job ads in newspapers and journals.

Bruce Tulgan

We have been told repeatedly that the traditional career is over. Most people believe it, but nobody really seems to know what is going to replace it. Bruce Tulgan's *Work this Way* is a guide to the post-jobs era that aims to provide a set of readily applicable strategies for prospering in an environment where many are intent on merely surviving.

Tulgan offers the five essential ingredients of a reinvented career:

1. **Learn voraciously** – the next generation of employees already has an insatiable appetite for information. According to Tulgan we need to:
    *   Create our own opportunities to learn – the traditional education system by itself is no longer enough
    *   Take personal control of our post-school education by designing our own courses
    *   Maximize all corporate training opportunities and turn everyday life into a learning lab
    *   Turn job-hopping into a personal training programme.

2. **Concentrate on relationships** – relationships with individuals will be the most reliable institutions in the post-jobs era. We need to:
    *   Identify and seek out the real decision-makers
    *   Turn every contact into a multiple contact
    *   Identify and win over gatekeepers
    *   Get on the right person's radar, *then prove that we are more than a blip*
    *   Take personal responsibility for keeping relationships fizzing.

3. **Add value continuously** – the most successful workers today are chameleon-like, day-to-day value adders who are flexible and adapt well to changing circumstances. There are temps – the fastest growing category of employees – but temping is not just for clerical workers anymore but for doctors, lawyers, engineers, bankers, scientists, teachers, programmers, trapeze artists and any other type of worker you can think of.

4. **Be balanced** – Tulgan urges us to set clear priorities in our working and personal lives and then to live by them no matter what. He considers it

essential to stay close to our deepest values and priorities such as quality, integrity, fulfilment and well being.

5. **Take it one year at a time** – in a changing environment long-term goals are good but long-term planning is useless. Instead Tulgan encourages us to plan our lives and careers only one year at a time.

Like Tom Peters, Tulgan fizzes with provocative ideas, and, like Peters, much of what he writes about will prove to be wrong. However, buried within *Work this Way* are some profound truths about the way things will be. The trick is to find them and to prepare ourselves accordingly. His latest book, *Winning the Talent Wars*, came out in the spring of 2001.

What has been lacking is a language to describe the skills and attributes associated with effective career management. We are familiar with the competencies that can be applied to the majority of job roles and professions. What has not been developed to date, at least to the best of my knowledge, is a set of competencies that apply specifically to the Smart Careerist. In other words, nobody has yet identified a set of explicit skills and characteristics deployed by people who are successful in building and sustaining their careers.

Until now.

(Sorry about that – probably a tad over-dramatic.)

In the rest of this section is a first stab at outlining 15 key competencies needed by the Smart Careerist. These competencies have been derived from a mixture of personal research, interviews with a number of successful business people, and published books and articles on the subject of career management.

That said, this list is not definitive. I would really welcome your comments, suggestions and feedback about the competency framework set out over the coming pages. In particular, I would love to hear from you if you believe there are important competencies missing from my list. You can contact me by e-mail on john@lifegym.co.uk

Introducing the Smart Careerist competency set

At its heart, having a smart career revolves around three main elements:

1. being highly competent (at the very least) at the work you do,

2. being highly skilled at ensuring that your genuine accomplishments are recognized and appreciated,

3. having clarity about what you are trying to achieve in career terms, and knowing who and what you need to know in order to get there.

Put together the skills and behaviours implicit behind these three elements and you have the basis of the Smart Careerist's competency set.

So what are the competencies for the Smart Careerist?

Here are the fifteen competencies that I believe are crucial to having a smart career:

1. Decision making

2. Networking

3. Thinking systemically

4. Handling information

5. Becoming a brilliant listener

6. Looking the part

7. Looking after yourself

8. Project management

9. Managing external consultants effectively

10. Being a good team player

11. Be emotionally intelligent

12. Being innovative

13. Leadership

14. Managing the brand called you

15. Making it happen

Let's explore them in a bit more detail. As we do this, though, please bear in mind this quote from Edward de Bono's book *Simplicity* (Penguin, 1999):

> Some rules do not have to be obeyed – but it is useful to keep them in mind. The purpose of a rule may be to remind us of what lies behind the rule.

1. DECISION MAKING

When making business decisions, 88% of management admit to using gut feel over and above hard facts up to 75% of the time. 91% admit that they do not get enough thinking time, and 62% say that they do not get the right amount of information to make a decision.

Decision Making Survey 1997 (Business Objects)

Decision-making has been defined as the ability to decide on a course of action after due reflection. Smart Careerists give themselves time to think, but don't procrastinate. Making good-quality decisions enables us to show that we can make a positive difference, that we are not merely intent on maintaining the *status quo*.

An article in *Fast Company* magazine (October 1998) suggests four steps to making smarter decisions:

1. Wait until the last minute – but not a minute later: If you're not going to do anything differently tomorrow by making a decision today, then don't make it today. Situations change; markets shift. That's not an excuse to procrastinate. But the best decisions are just-in-time decisions. You should decide as late as possible – but before you need to take action.

2. Don't be afraid to argue: Conflict is good for an organization – as long as it's resolved quickly. Unresolved conflict is a killer. That's why real leaders deal with conflict head-on.

SMART VOICES

If you can talk brilliantly about a problem, it can create the consoling illusion that it has been mastered.

Stanley Kubrick

They take individual feelings seriously, but then they get beyond those feelings. One way to make progress on a tough decision is to agree on what the question is. Agree on the wording and write it down. Debate often stems from having different ideas about what's being decided.

3. Make the right decision, not the best decision: People can spend months debating the 'best' decision without actually arriving at any decision. Every decision involves risk. And if there are 10 ways to do something, 8 of them will probably work. So pick one of the 8 and get going. Life's too short. You have 10 more decisions to make after this one.

4. Disagree – and then commit: Not everyone gets a chance to decide, but everyone should have a chance to be heard. Without at doubt, the most vigorous debates yield the best thinking. But once a decision is made, you should not be able to tell who was for it and who was against it. Fully supporting decisions that have been properly made is a condition of employment.

SMART VOICES

In a Harvard Business School article entitled "The Hidden Traps in Decision Making", John S. Hammond, Ralph L. Keeney and Howard Raiffa maintain that bad decisions can often be traced back to the way the decisions were made. For example, perhaps the alternatives were not clearly defined, the right information was not collected, the costs and benefits were not accurately weighed. But sometimes the fault lies not in the decision-making process but rather in the mind of the decision-maker. The way the human brain works can sabotage the choices we make.

Here are eight psychological traps that Hammond, Keeney and Raiffa believe are particularly likely to affect the way people make business decisions:

1. The anchoring trap: this leads us to give disproportionate weight to the first information we receive.

2. The status-quo trap: this biases us toward maintaining the current situation – even when better alternatives exist.

3. The sunk-cost trap: this inclines us to perpetuate the mistakes of the past.

4. The confirming-evidence trap: this leads us to seek out information supporting an existing predilection and to discount opposing information.

5. The framing trap: this occurs when we misstate a problem, undermining the entire decision-making process.

6. The overconfidence trap: this makes us overestimate the accuracy of our forecasts.

7. The prudence trap: this leads us to be overcautious when we make estimates about uncertain events.

8. The recallability trap: this leads us to give undue weight to recent, dramatic events.

2. NETWORKING

ETH: *If Ron doesn't mix with better-class people, how's he going to get on in life? In this world, it's not what you know, it's who you know, isn't it Ron?*

RON: *Yes Eth, And I don't know either of them.*

Frank Muir and Denis Norden, The Glums,
Take It From Here, BBC Radio

In 1960, the average manager had to learn 25 names throughout their entire career; today we must learn 25 new names every single month. Tomorrow, it may be 25 new names per week.

Jonas Ridderstråle & Kjell Nordström, *Funky Business*

If you want to change jobs, forget rifling through the recruitment advertisements in the newspapers and journals. Research by Coutts Consultants suggests that as many as two-thirds of all job moves come about on the back of networking.

Networking has been defined as "all the different ways in which people make, and are helped to make, connections with each other". It sometimes gets a bad press from those who see networking as replicating the exclusiveness of old boy networks. However, as traditional formal hierarchies disappear and professionals become increasingly mobile, networking has become ever more important.

There are four main types of network:

**Smart things
to say about your career**

It's not what you know, it's who you know. Work is social. Career success depends more on your network than on your work.

- *Personal*, e.g. friends, relations, neighbours.

- *Work*, e.g. present and past bosses and colleagues, former clients or suppliers

- *Professionals*, e.g. solicitors, accountants, bank managers (do they still exist?), shop owners, doctors

- *Organizations*, e.g. professional associations, clubs chamber of commerce, clubs you belong to

Here are six tips on how to network to best effect:

1. It takes time and effort to develop your network. You can't live in a house until it's built, and you can't make use of a network until you've put one in place. To quote the title of a book on networking by Harvey Mackay, *Dig Your Well Before You're Thirsty*.

2. A good network requires active attention. Just because you have somebody's business card tucked away in a desk drawer doesn't necessarily mean they're part of your network. The acid test is whether you could pick up the phone and call them right now without them taking umbrage. Put it another way: if you got a call from a fellow delegate on a course you went on ten years ago and you could barely remember them, how much help realistically would you want to be to them? As a general guide, if you haven't had any contact with somebody for at least six months, it may be presumptuous to assume they're part of your network.

3. Before you start actively using your network, be absolutely clear what you're trying to achieve. If you want to put the word out that you are looking to change jobs, remember that the more focused the message you feed into a network, the better the chance that something might come of it. "I'm looking for a senior sales role in pharmaceuticals" is far more likely to register with people than "I'm

KILLER QUESTIONS

Could you diversify your contacts? Why not aim to double the number of contacts you have over the next six months?

just ready to move on, maybe into consultancy, maybe into another senior business development role. Not really bothered a which industry sector."

4. Enlist people to your cause – don't put them on the defensive by appearing to exploit your relationship with them. It's far more effective to ask people for their advice and guidance than to ask them outright for a job.

5. Widen your network by using existing contacts to give you the names of other useful people.

6. Remember to keep a record of who you contact. When somebody gives you their business card, jot down on the back of the card where and when you met them.

Work increasingly consists of talk. In the old days, they used to have notices in factories saying, Talk less, Work more. But today, try ringing someone at the office, and they're always at a meeting. Go to a doctor's surgery, and watch how getting a diagnosis is now only a part of a medical consultation: doctors are expected to engage in a conversation between equals, in which the patient has as much right to question and demand as the doctor. In retailing, sales-people are trained not so much to obey orders as to talk to customers with a smile. Everywhere, the higher you climb up in the hierarchy, the more time you spend discussing. There are very few supreme heights left where you need listen only to your own voice.

Theodore Zeldin, from An Intimate History of Conversation, Radio 4, 16 March 1998

3. THINKING SYSTEMICALLY

Systems thinking is a discipline for seeing wholes. It is a framework for seeing inter-relationships rather than things, for seeing patterns of change rather than static snapshots.

Peter Senge, The Fifth Discipline

Any idea is a feat of association.

Robert Frost

The Smart Careerist who can think systemically can distinguish themselves in two ways: (1) by producing better-quality thinking – and hence better quality decisions – in the workplace; and (2) by using systems thinking principles to take a more creative approach to their career management.

Picture the scene: you stroll into your local bookstore and catch sight of a forward-thinking work colleague of yours. (Alright, I know that "forward-thinking" may not be the adjective that comes most readily to mind as a way to describe the people you work alongside, and I accept that "colleague" might be more than you would readily admit to in public, but bear with me . . .). The point I want to make is about where in the bookshop you are most likely to spot them – these days the chances are they're to be found poring over the latest additions to the science section rather than clutching a trendy management tome.

This is because more and more management thinkers and writers are suggesting that scientific theory is a prime source for understanding how organizations and individuals can improve their performance.

This in itself is nothing new. In fact, an overt relationship between business and science dates back at least to the beginning of the last century, when Frederick Taylor, engineer and inventor, and originator of what became known as the school of Scientific Management, set out to identify what he called the "single best way" to carry out jobs. This process involved breaking work down into discrete tasks that could be done by the most unskilled workers. In so doing, Taylor lay the ground for the mass production techniques that dominated management thinking in the first half of the twentieth century.

Most recently, it has been the field of complexity science, sometimes known as chaos theory, which has captured the corporate imagination.

Complexity science is huge in its scope and, well yes, it's quite complex to grasp. You can all too easily get bound up in the technical terminology – phrases like "strange attractors", "emergent capabilities", "states of disequilibrium" etc. abound in the complexity textbooks. At its heart though is the deceptively simple principle that an entity needs to be looked at as a whole "living" system, rather than as a set of individual components.

This insight raises a host of fascinating questions about how we should be tackling the problems we face in organizations. For instance, when analysing an organizational issue, we have the option of exploring it at a number of levels. Experts suggest that there are at least eight, namely:

1. Individual

2. Team

3. Inter-group

4. Organizational

5. Inter-organizational

6. Societal

7. International

8. Global

Let's take a recent example, the general débâcle formerly known as the American presidential race. Among the reasons cited, and depending on who you listened to, you could have analysed the problem at the level of:

1. voters who were "too stupid to vote properly" (i.e. at the Individual level);

2. lack of agreed standards about how to count votes (i.e. an Inter-group problem);

3. badly designed voting cards (i.e. an Organizational issue); or

4. inherent flaws in the whole electoral system (i.e. at the Societal level)

Why does this matter? The point is that the level of explanation that we choose determines our view of the causes of an event or problem. It also affects the actions that we take, and the solutions that we employ. In an organization, an inappropriate intervention at the wrong level can make a problem worse and not better.

Virtual working will mean employees taking responsibility for delivering to a specification, rather than putting in a quantum of time. People will come to like this; they will not be impressed with presenteeism.

Valerie Bayliss, Director of the RSA's Redefining Work project, interviewed in *People Management*, 30 April 1998

Three other points to consider:

- People tend to pick their favourite level of analysis to explain events, and then behave accordingly. This is often particularly true of external consultants by the way.

- People are most familiar with, and often prefer, explanations at the individual level of behaviour. Trying to change people by sending them on a training course is simpler than changing structures or upgrading technology. However, such explanations all too often are simplistic, inaccurate or incomplete.

- As a general principle, any organizational problem, for example low productivity or poor team performance, can usefully be analysed at ever-higher levels of abstraction. By considering it progressively at the individual, group, inter-group and organization levels, a deeper understanding of its causes can be gained. As a result, the tools needed to tackle the problem can be chosen more accurately, and applied more effectively.

Looking at a problem "systemically", to use the jargon, will always yield a better understanding than simply leaping in with all preconceptions blazing. So in future, before we too hastily attribute a train crash to "driver error", perhaps we ought to bear in mind the impact of lack of investment in the railway infrastructure. Before we blame a member of staff for cocking up a customer order, maybe we need to ask ourselves whether it truly was their fault. And next time you chance upon a management colleague in the science section of Waterstones, don't be concerned – they're just trying to improve their own and your company's performance.

4. HANDLING INFORMATION

> *The average Briton is exposed to around 2,500 advertising messages a day.*
>
> *The Observer*, 16 January 2000

With advance apologies for some gratuitous name-dropping, Tom Peters, co-author of *In Search of Excellence* and probably the best-known management guru of them all, told me something startling a few months back:

> I am finding the last eighteen months with this Internet thing so exhausting to keep up. . . . I didn't have a bad time five years ago but now it's awful. I feel the weight of it on me as I sort through magazines, patrol 15 or 20 bookmarked sites on the web every night and it just feels like . . . if I retire it will be because of the burden.

Information overload is one of the less attractive by-products of the knowledge economy. When I last checked, there were over 15 million websites out there, and literally thousands of magazines and books published every week. Add to that the growth in use of e-mail; garnish with a sizeable pile of junk mail, and small wonder that it's a struggle for us to deal with it all without screaming.

Overload can cause stress, which leads to a feeling of strain, and, of course, mistakes are more likely to occur when we're under extreme pressure. And a reputation for making mistakes is definitely not what a smart careerist wants.

Having a Smart Career means keeping aware of the latest trends affecting your chosen profession; it means knowing which job websites specialize in your field; it means knowing when your professional association is holding meetings in your region; it means maintaining a list of useful people to know. It means, in short, know what is relevant and what isn't.

It is the irrelevant that clutters up our lives. Here then are a few ideas for clearing excess data out of your life:

1. Set your e-mail program to filter your e-mails.

2. Tear out the magazine articles and newsletters that you really want to read and throw away the rest of the publication. That way, you don't risk unintentionally reading the same useless stuff again.

3. Train yourself to ignore junk e-mails and unsolicited messages. You might miss something but in the long run you'll be more focused and effective.

4. Don't leave a message sitting in your inbox – take action on it immediately so as not to open the same messages more than once.

5. Learn how to use search engines efficiently. Most have help sections that will teach you how to search to best effect.

6. Where possible, go for the "edited highlights" rather than the "live transmission". Avoid attending meetings where possible – make do with reading the minutes. A friend of mine once calculated that an hour of meeting time could easily be distilled into notes that take one minute to read.

7. And finally a broader point. Physical clutter is a constant distraction. Keep your work area clear of jumbled up piles. Don't simply file stuff away or put it in a drawer – the goal is to have less around in.

Here are five ways not to contribute to other people's information overload:

1. Think about how best to contact someone. Is the information best delivered as a voicemail message, an e-mail, or a fax? Or can you just drop it in the post?

2. Write economically and concisely. Being verbose wastes everyone's time.

3. Change the words in the subject field of an e-mail. This helps suggest how the conversation has moved on, so the recipient can decide whether to read the message now, later, or at all.

4. Do not forward chain letters or claims that Bill Gates will send everyone thousands of dollars. These things clog up inboxes with worthless stuff.

5. Check the 'To:' field of your e-mails. Do all the named recipients really need to see your message?

Source: *The Observer*, 16 January 2000

> Smart things to say about your career

5. BECOME A BRILLIANT LISTENER

He knew the precise psychological moment when to say nothing.
Oscar Wilde, *The Picture of Dorian Gray*

Being smart at work is certainly about what you do, but it's also about how much you take in. Being alert to the thoughts, feelings and ideas of others enables you to come up with better quality solutions. Taking time to listen enables you to satisfy your curiosity, to get another point of view, and to be better informed.

KILLER QUESTIONS

How often do you interrupt other people before they have finished their point? How in turn do you feel about being interrupted when you're in full flow?

Good listening skills are the bedrock of good decision making, effective networking, seeing the big picture, managing information, etc. In fact, it is impossible to be capable at the first four competencies if you don't have the ability to listen.

Listening with undivided attention is also the key to making the most of any feedback you are given by others. Feedback can improve the way you manage your day-to-day performance or your broader career, and it can be found almost anytime, anywhere – if you're prepared to look out for it

Nancy Kline

Over the past 17 years, Nancy Kline has developed a system called a Thinking Environment™, a model of human interaction that dramatically improves the way people think – and thus work and live. Listening – defined by Kline as the quality of people's attention for each other – is the core of this method. Here, in a brief extract from her book *Time to Think*, is an example of how people, when managed effectively, can talk themselves into lucidity:

> Organizations intimidate people into believing that "the higher up you are in a hierarchy, the better you can think". And welding this assumption to the floor of the mind of managers is the assumption that to seek out ideas from people junior to you is to look incompetent. The absurdity of this is obvious – often the people near the top, because of their isolation from what is really happening, have less chance of thinking well than most of the people junior to them – but the assumption persists nevertheless.
>
> Not, however, at Staples, the office supplies company. One of the divisional managers has done a good thing. She has institutionalized equality of thinking in the work place. She has set up a forum for ideas, a bi-monthly meeting with all levels of her staff. She gathers them in groups of about twelve (which, by the way, is about as big as you can make a group and still expect it to be safe enough for people to say what they think. Organizations that gather two hundred employees to announce policy changes and then open the floor to questions and comments from the audience are, in effect, not holding an open consultative forum at all. Most people will not stand up to speak in a group of colleagues that large).

SMART
PEOPLE
TO HAVE
ON YOUR
SIDE

The Staples manager poses two questions:

1. What have you noticed that needs attention or change in this company that I might not have noticed?

2. What do you think should be done about it?

Then she sits down and listens. Everyone speaks without rush or interruption. She makes notes, asks clarifying questions only, does not challenge their ideas or defend herself She promises to think about each one. She does not promise to do everything people suggest, but she does agree to let them know what she decides to do with their ideas and why. This takes time, but she claims it has gained time overall because embers have been snuffed before they combusted, new paths she had never thought of have opened up, and employee involvement and commitment have increased – those two unmeasurable soft qualities on which so much of the hard stuff depends.

Equality is particularly a feature in any Thinking Environment meeting. Many times during the meeting, including at the beginning and at the end, everyone has a turn to speak. Every person is considered equally valuable. The chair or other people in authority may have to make the final decisions; not every meeting can work effectively on consensus. But the chance to contribute ideas and points of view is given equally in a Thinking Environment.

This seems basic and obvious to me. If you value only certain people's ideas, don't invite the others to the meeting. And if you don't want anyone's ideas, issue a memo and save everyone a lot of time and degradation. But if you want ideas better than your own and a meeting with better and better concrete outcomes and a team that works splendidly together, invite them all and give everyone an uninterrupted turn to speak and the skills to listen. Every Team Start-up Kit should have this right on the top.

Seeing people as thinking equals makes them functionally more clever. The things you learn and the more competent you become by hearing their thinking makes listening to people as equals almost a selfish act. There is so much in it for you.

Taken from *Time to Think* by Nancy Kline (Ward Lock, 1999)

6. LOOKING THE PART

The workplace is rife with people who are paid very well for doing their jobs badly and others who are poorly paid for doing their jobs brilliantly.

Neasa MacErlean, *Get More from Work – And More Fun*

Physical appearance counts in the workplace, according to a US survey. People rated as attractive are two to five times more likely to be taken on. They are also less likely to be laid off.

The Guardian, 25 March 2000

A study of 350 firms in Italy has found that employees, female and male alike, tend to work better, and are more prepared to put in longer hours, if they are working for a good looking, well groomed boss.

Daily Telegraph, 18 September 2000

Half the population meet their future partner at work.

Survey by Industrial Society, April 1998

Next time you write a report, will you write a better one if you are smartly dressed? Will you be more likely to meet your deadlines? Will you return phone calls and e-mails more promptly? If you are investigating something, will your jeans and tennis shoes cause you to get the facts wrong?

Probably not. And yet a recent report by the Industrial Society called "Looking Good, Sounding Right? Style Counselling in the New Economy" recommended that ambitious executives should spend less time working and more time grooming themselves. Although it may not be that palatable in these politically correct times, there is ample evidence to suggest that career success is more likely to go to those who look and dress the part.

Appearance does seem to matter, beyond the need to make a good first impression on business associates, customers, and friends. A professional appearance means you are more apt to act professional and be more productive in a business environment. The BBC used to make all their on-air talent dress in formal clothes, including black tie, even though these people were on the radio where no one saw them. The reason was that if people dress formally, they act formally.

> ### Smart things
> ### to say about your career
>
> Your home or your office is your visual autobiography. If visitors think your abode is disorganized, then chances are that they will think the same of you.

More recently, the introduction of "dressing down" to a "business casual" dress code has raised tricky problems. In a recent article in the *Financial Times*, one company spokesperson warned that if someone fails to apply what is seen as sensible judgment about dress, this affects management's view of that person's overall judgement.

Perhaps what we wear at work will have diminishing importance in the years ahead. Martin Raymond, a senior lecturer at the London School of Fashion, predicted in an interview published in *The Times* (8 October 2000) that "the three-piece suit will die off because there is a generation which thinks suits represents an authority it doesn't trust". For now though, the Smart Careerist needs to think very carefully about what they pluck from the wardrobe before heading off to work.

Keep your hair on

Two research studies have found that bald men have less chance of successfully changing jobs than their hirsute colleagues. Researchers created six fictitious CVs, three featuring photographs of men with hair, and three giving the same biographical information and showing the same three men, but with their image digitally altered to make them bald. The CVs were then sent to a total of 98 personnel managers along with a batch of genuine applications. Only 27% of the "bald" candidates were invited to interview, compared with 41% of those with hair.

Daily Express, 2 May 2000

Here's the deal on men and ties. 98% of men are heavier than they were when they were 20, and instead of admitting it and trying to lose the weight or admitting it and starting to buy shirts with a slightly larger collar size, they stubbornly buy the same collar size they wore 25 years ago even if it cuts off all circulation to their brain.

An image consultant, who contributed to a recent web discussion of the importance of appearance

7. LOOK AFTER YOURSELF

Sustaining a Smart Career takes commitment and it takes energy. In order to look and feel the part, you need to look after your general health. The two key ingredients to a healthy life are healthy eating and exercise.

Healthy eating

The basis of healthy eating is very simple. There are five simple rules:

1. Over half of your diet should be made up of complex carbohydrates. These are foods such as bread, cereals, rice, pasta, etc. If you can, try to eat the wholewheat and wholemeal varieties, because these are high in fibre and are nearer to food in its natural state.

2. Eat less fat. In general you should try and eat less than 30% of your diet as fat, especially saturated animal fats. For weight loss you should try to decrease your fat intake to 20%.

3. Eat less sugar. Sugar is just empty calories and has no nutritional value whatsoever.

4. Eat more fruit and vegetables. Aim for at least five portions a day.

5. Change the basis of meals. Instead of meat and two veg the everyday norm for main meals should be bread, potatoes, rice or pasta with plenty of vegetables or salad. You can include a little lean meat or fish if you wish, but the emphasis should be on the carbohydrates.

Exercise

Despite the exhortations of doctors and other health professionals, an estimated 75% of the UK adult population do not exercise enough to show a health benefit. And this is before the full sedentary impact of the knowledge economy is felt.

There are a number of merits to taking regular exercise. The psychological benefits are that exercise:

- Improves sense of well-being and enhances self-image

- Decreases anxiety and tension

- Reduces depression

- Increases self-efficacy and self-confidence

- Enhances adherence to weight control behaviors

The health benefits of exercise include a decreased resting heart rate, reduced blood pressure, and improved insulin sensitivity.

KILLER QUESTION

When did you last have a health screen?

8. PROJECT MANAGEMENT

As the pace of organizational change becomes ever more headlong, companies are increasingly using a project-based approach to deliver rapid results. Having highly developed project management skills provides an opportunity for the Smart Careerist to shine in what are often high-profile situations. It also provides a useful methodology and set of tools for addressing personal career issues.

At its core, project management is simply the planning, organizing, and managing of tasks and resources to accomplish a defined objective, usually with constraints on time and cost.

The 10 Laws of Project Management

1. No major project is ever installed on time, within budget or with the same staff that started it. Yours will not be the first.

2. The first 90 percent of the project takes 90 percent of the time. The last 10 percent takes the other 90 percent.

3. When things are going well, something will go wrong.

4. When things can't get any worse, they will.

5. When things appear to be going better, you have overlooked something.

6. A carelessly planned project will take three times longer to complete than expected. A carefully planned project will take only twice as long.

7. Plagiarism is copying from one source. Research is copying from two or more.

8. The light at the end of the tunnel is the headlight of the oncoming train.

9. If it's stupid but it works, it isn't stupid.

10. In a critical and visible project, anything you do can get you fired, including nothing.

Source: Unknown, frequently circulated on the Internet

A project plan can be as simple as a list of tasks and their scheduled start and finish dates. A complex plan, on the other hand, might deal with thousands of tasks and resources and a project budget of millions of pounds. Most project plans share some common elements, including breaking the project into easily manageable tasks, scheduling the tasks, and then tracking the tasks as work progresses.

There are two key phases in this process:

1. Planning the project and creating a schedule

This is the most important phase of project management. It includes defining tasks and their durations, setting up relationships between tasks, and assigning resources. All of the project's later phases are based directly on the information you use when planning your project.

It's vital to have as much clarity as possible about project goals – the better defined they are, they greater likelihood of a successful outcome for the project. Before you invoke the mental image of albumen and yolk dribbling down your grandmother's chin in the middle of her egg-sucking lesson, I would point out that in my experience of project management absolute clarity of purpose is a regularly missing ingredient. Common sense is very different from common practice. Here are some of the misconceptions that can undermine a project at birth:

• The belief that senior managers give a lot of thought to what they want from a project before they give it to the project leader.

- The belief that the senior manager's definition of the problem or solution should be accepted because he/she has thought about it or has more experience.

- The belief by senior managers that what is obvious to them must be obvious to the project leader or project team.

- The belief that project clients ought to have a clear idea of what they want.

- The belief that terms of reference only need to be in writing to be understood.

Having a clear, quantifiable goal for a project helps enormously. "Climb hill to the summit within two hours spending less than £10" is a lot better than "Go for a nice walk". Similarly, "Increase my network of contacts by 50% within six months" is an improvement over "Must try to get out more".

2. Managing changes

This phase of project management is an ongoing process that begins once you create a schedule and ends when the project is complete. Managing a project includes tracking and adjusting your schedule to reflect changes that occur as the project progresses.

There are a number of project "time stealers" that can throw everything off kilter:

- Communication issues – e.g. the process of informing people, helping them to understand, updating them and getting feedback, and reviewing.

- Key decision milestones outside your control – e.g. gaining approval for a primary project element at a board meeting or a particular committee. If you miss a specific meeting, there is often not another one for months.

- The difficulty of organizing meetings involving several busy people.

- The need for end users to be brought up to date and perhaps trained.

- Assembling all the resources you need.

KILLER QUESTIONS

If you could work on any project in your company, which one would it be? If you have any choice in the matter, here are six questions worth asking before you commit yourself:

1. What can I learn?
2. What can I contribute?
3. Who is leading the project?
4. How important is the project?
5. Does the project have a high profile?
6. If it goes well, will I get noticed?

9. MANAGING EXTERNAL CONSULTANTS EFFECTIVELY

These days, organizations are bringing in external consultants in ever-increasing numbers, particularly against a background of more and more activities being out-sourced. This being so, the ability to make best and most cost-effective use of consultants becomes crucial. Smart Careerists know that their personal reputation is on the line every time they are responsible for managing the performance of external consultants.

Here are some guidelines on how best to manage consultants, derived from *Dangerous Company* by James O'Shea and Charles Madigan:

1. Why are you doing this? Before you sit down to talk to a consulting firm, it would help to have some idea of what it is you want to achieve. The more clearly the goal is defined, the greater the chance of reaching it. If you don't know what you want to do, don't make the call.

2. Having determined the goal, ask yourself whether you really need outsiders to help you reach it. Don't forget to assess the brilliance within your own company before you go trying to buy some from outside. Maybe you don't need an army of consultants. Maybe you just need your very own MBA, whom you can easily steal from a consulting company.

3. If you hire a consulting company which characters will they send? Be ruthless in this part of the process. If you know the reputations of the partners, or if they display a special, tested expertise, demand that they personally pay good and frequent attention to your needs. Make it a part of the contract. If they are promising the best, make certain that is what shows up, and not an army of their latest graduate intake. Send away people who make you uncomfortable.

4. What will it cost? (And how long will it take?) Avoid open-ended arrangements and vague promises. Go instead for specificity in contracts, including the dark parts about what happens if the consulting engagement doesn't work. Be tight with your money. Base pay-

ments on performance and on your satisfaction. If the task involves high risk, make certain the consulting company is sharing in the risk, not just in the rewards, of the relationship.

5. Never give up control. The best consulting engagements do not take over your operations, they complement them. Make certain your own people retain control over everything, share in decision-making, and understand that for the duration of the contract, they are responsible and in charge.

6. Consultants can shower down all kinds of havoc on a company. If you sense something is going wrong, confront it immediately and demand repairs. Consultants don't answer to boards of directors, but you do. At these prices, happiness should be assumed.

7. Beware of glib talkers with books. The fact that someone can stack up case after case in which a practice seemed to work is no guarantee it will work for you. Insist on tailor-made consulting engagements that recognize the unique nature of your business. Don't be afraid to trim elegant proposals right down to their essence.

8. Value your employees. One of the most common complaints about consultants is that they talk down to the locals or ignore their ideas. Long after the consultants leave, your staff will be on board. How they feel about the outsiders has a lot to do with whether the engagement will work. The best consulting companies know this and will go to great lengths to avoid morale problems. You are buying intelligence, not arrogance.

9. Measure the process. Make certain you have your own internal measure of how a procedure is progressing. Consulting companies do, and they generally try to make this a part of the process.

10. If it's not broke, don't try to fix it. This is a great cliché, but more than an afterthought. It is in the consulting company's interest to find trouble where you see calm waters. The consultant's goal will be to sell much broader involvement than you might want or need. It is part of their nature. But it doesn't have to be part of yours.

Here is an infallible rule: a prince who is not himself wise cannot be wisely advised. . . . Good advice depends on the shrewdness of the prince who seeks it, and not the shrewdness of the prince on good advice.

Niccolò Machiavelli, *The Prince*

10. BE A GOOD TEAM PLAYER

The Smart Careerist recognizes that for most of us in organizations, success often depends on surrounding yourself with the very best people. Working collaboratively is far more likely to deliver good results than working competitively. Somebody once wrote that moving from dependence to independence is a sign of growing up, but that moving from independence to interdependence is a sign of maturity.

There was a story in the papers about four years ago concerning one of the main Whitehall departments that used to run a course called "Getting the Most Out of Your Junior Staff". One of the juniors objected to the title and as a consequence the course was renamed "Succeeding with Teams". The content, needless to say, was identical.

If nothing else, this anecdote serves to demonstrate how potent the concept of "team" has become in recent times. There are plenty of books on the market that look at how teams can operate to best effect – I'd particularly commend another book from this series, *Smart Things to Know about Teams* by Annemarie Caracciolo, if you want to explore this subject in depth. I'll therefore concentrate in this section on some of the things that Smart Careerists can do to optimize their relationship with other team members. There are three areas in particular I'd like to highlight:

1. *Giving team members undivided attention*

2. *Giving team members unexpected attention*

3. *Avoiding the things that irritate team members*

1. The best compliment you can pay co-workers is to give them your absolute undivided attention. Show you're interested. Show that you remember what people tell you. I have an acquaintance who maintains a database of over 3,000 people, with information on birthdays, names of family members, last time they spoke, etc. Whether you regard this as commendably organized or faintly sinister is not the point (and be aware of the Data Protection Act). The fact is people like to be recognized and remembered.

2. Try giving a colleague some unexpected attention – a card, a smile, a cake. Just to be clear, we are talking something good with no strings

attached, not a suggestive item from the Ann Summers catalogue for the person in Accounts that you've taken a shine to.

3. A couple of years back, a survey by Office Angels identified what irritated people most in the modern office. The top five were: colleagues leaving mobile phones on in meetings; leaving the office photocopier jammed or out of paper; people talking loudly; gossiping or spreading rumours; and taking other people's stationery without asking.

SMART
PEOPLE
TO HAVE
ON YOUR
SIDE

Jon R. Katzenbach

Co-author of *The Wisdom of Teams*, perhaps the most influential book about teams published in the last decade, Jon Katzenbach has in recent times moved his focus up the organizational ladder.

Katzenbach believes that the best corporate leaders are those who actively shift in and out of team mode behind closed doors. The widely held view that teamwork is a *sine qua non* of organizational success is, he believes, fundamentally mistaken and has generated five myths about teamwork at the top, namely that:

1. Teamwork at the top will lead to team performance.
2. Top teams need to spend more time together building consensus.
3. CEOs must change their personal style to obtain team performance.
4. The senior group should function as a team whenever it is together.
5. Teams at the top need to "set the example".

He maintains that the challenge for executives is to see through these myths and recognize when a team effort is needed and when a working group under single leadership is the more effective route to follow.

Paradoxically, in an article titled "How Management Teams Can Have a Good Fight" by Eisenhardt, Kahwajy and Bourgeois (*Harvard Business Review*, July–August 1997), it was suggested that constructive conflict can actually enhance team performance and in turn achieve better decision making. The authors suggested five ways to achieve this:

1. Assemble a team with diverse ages, backgrounds and industry experience.

2. Meet frequently to build familiarity and mutual confidence.

3. Encourage team members to assume roles outside of their obvious functional responsibilities, and so discourage "turf war" thinking.

4. Apply multiple perspectives – role playing, putting yourself in the competitor's shoes etc. This can enable a fresh view of the problem.

5. Actively and overtly manage conflict Ensure that consensus is real and not just an indication of disengagement.

I don't want any yes-men around me. I want everybody to tell me the truth even if it costs them their jobs.

Movie mogul Samuel Goldwyn

SMART QUOTES

In her book *Team Talk: The Power of Language in Team Dynamics* (Harvard Business School Press, 1996), Anne Donnellon uses anthropological and linguistic research techniques to focus on talk as the "medium through which team work is done and through which organizational and individual forces can be observed and analysed". Given that language exchange is the primary way in which people swap information, make decisions and formulate plans, Donnellon's book represents the long overdue entry of sociolinguistics into the field of management studies.

She looks at a team's use of language through six dimensions:

1. Identification: e.g. use of terms like "we" or "us" to describe the team.

2. Interdependence: e.g. explicit references to independence or interdependence.

3. Power differentiation: e.g. challenges, corrections, verbal aggression, apologies.

4. Social distance: e.g. formal forms of address (Mr Blair or Tony), use of slang, nicknames.

5. Conflict management tactics: e.g. use of confrontational, accommodating or avoidance language.

6. Negotiation process: e.g. use of win–win and win–lose language.

What emerges clearly from her work is a sense of the significant extent to which the language used by teams both reflects and indeed shapes relationships within and outside the team.

Team Talk is a detailed study of an under-explored topic and as such requires more concentration than many recent books on teams. It is somewhat academic in tone, but the effort needed to read it is certainly repaid.

11. BE EMOTIONALLY INTELLIGENT

A Prayer for the Stressed

Grant me the serenity to accept the things I cannot change, the courage to change the things I cannot accept and the wisdom to hide the bodies of those that I had to kill today because they got on my nerves!

Also, help me to be careful of the toes I step on today as they may be connected to the feet I may have to kiss tomorrow.

Help me to always give 100% at work:

12% on Monday
23% on Tuesday
40% on Wednesday
20% on Thursday
and 5% on Friday

And help me to remember, when I am having a bad day and it seems that people are trying to wind me up, that it takes 42 muscles to frown, 28 to smile and only 4 to extend my arm and smack someone in the mouth.

Anon., currently being circulated around the Web

You're not paranoid – you're the opposite of paranoid. You suffer from the insane delusion that people actually like you.

Woody Allen in *Deconstructing Harry* (1998)

> ## SMART QUOTES
>
> He who digs a hole for another may fall in it himself.
>
> Russian proverb

Emotional intelligence refers to the capacity for recognizing our own feelings and those of others, for motivating ourselves, and for managing emotions in ourselves and in our relationships. It describes abilities distinct from, but complementary to academic intelligence. The emotionally intelligent Smart Careerist finds it easier to network than his or her emotionally unintelligent peers, easier to build effective team relationships, and easier to acknowledge and deal with constructive criticism of his or her performance.

According to Daniel Goleman, the main popularizer of the concept, Emotional intelligence embraces five emotional and social competencies:

1. **Self-awareness:** knowing what we are feeling in the moment and using those preferences to guide our decision-making

2. **Self-regulation:** handling our emotions so that they facilitate rather than interfere with the task in hand

3. **Motivation:** using our deepest preferences to move and guide us toward our goals

4. **Empathy:** sensing what others are feeling, being able to take their perspective and cultivating rapport with a broad range of people

5. **Social skills:** handling emotions in relationships well and accurately reading social situations and networks; interacting smoothly; using these skills to persuade, lead, negotiate and settle disputes, etc.

Here are some facts about lies taken from an article in *Time* magazine (13th March 2000)

- The average person is lied to about 200 times a day.
- 41% of lies seek to conceal misbehaviour ("Yes, I was working late last night"), while another 14% are those white lies that make social life manageable ("We would love to come to dinner tomorrow night but unfortunately we've got something else on.")
- Men lie roughly 20% more than women, but women are better at it
- The Japanese are the world's least comfortable fibbers – Russians are the most habitual liars.

There are, he writes in his book *Working with Emotional Intelligence* (Bloomsbury, 1998), a number of widespread misunderstandings about emotional intelligence:

First, emotional intelligence does not mean merely 'being nice'. At strategic moments, it may demand confronting someone with an uncomfortable but consequential truth they've been avoiding.

Second, emotional intelligence does not mean giving free rein to feelings – "letting it all hang out". Rather, it means managing feelings so that they are expressed appropriately and effectively, enabling people to work together smoothly toward their common goals.

Also, women are not "smarter" than men when it comes to emotional intelligence, nor are men superior to women. Each of us has a personal profile of strengths and weaknesses. Some of us may be highly empathic but lack some abilities to handle our own distress; others may be quite aware of the subtlest shift in our own moods, yet be inept socially.

It is true that men and women as groups tend to have a shared, gender-specific profile of strong and weak points. An analysis of emotional intelligence in thousands of men and women found that women, on average, are more aware of their emotions, show more empathy, and are more adept interpersonally. Men, on the other hand, are more self-confident and optimistic, adapt more easily, and handle stress better.

In general, however, there are far more similarities than differences. Some men are as empathic as the most interpersonally sensitive women, while some women are every bit as able to withstand stress as the most emotionally resilient men. Indeed, on average, looking at the overall ratings for men and women, the strengths and weaknesses average out, so that in terms of total emotional intelligence, there are no sex differences.

Finally, our level of emotional intelligence is not fixed genetically, nor does it develop only in early childhood. Unlike IQ, which changes little after our teen years, emotional intelligence continues to develop as we go through life and learn from our experiences. Studies that have tracked people's level of emotional intelligence through the years show that people get better and better in these

SMART VOICES

In many organizations, emotional intelligence is more noticeable by its absence than anything. Where people are not being emotionally intelligent, what you can see most commonly are individuals obsessively pursuing their own agendas. Self-interest rules.

In her brilliant book *Territorial Games* (Amacom, 1998), Annette Simmons explores the antithesis of emotionally intelligent behaviour by identifying ten of the games that people play to shore up their personal and corporate fiefdoms:

1. **Occupation:** marking territory; monopolizing resources, relationships or information
2. **Information manipulation:** withholding, covering up or giving false information
3. **Intimidation:** yelling; staring someone down; making threats (veiled or overt)
4. **Powerful alliances:** using relationships with powerful people to intimidate; name dropping
5. **Invisible wall:** discreetly creating perceptions that undermine previous agreements
6. **Strategic non-compliance:** agreeing to take action with no intention of acting
7. **Discredit:** using personal attacks to undermine the reputation or credibility of others
8. **Shunning:** personally exclude an individual; influence a group to treat another as an outsider
9. **Camouflage:** creating distractions; deliberately triggering anxiety in others
10. **Filibuster:** using excessive verbiage to prevent action; wearing others down by out-talking them

capabilities as they grow more adept at handling their own emotions and impulses, at motivating themselves, and at honing their empathy and social adroitness. There is an old-fashioned word for this growth in emotional intelligence: maturity.

12. INNOVATE

For the Smart Careerist, innovation should be a way of life. In a working world that grows ever more unpredictable, success will inevitably go to people who are naturally curious, willing to experiment, passionate about their work, and revolutionary in their thinking. Assuming that what works today will work tomorrow is a recipe for the scrapheap.

When it comes to assessing the contribution that his staff make to the business, Michael Eisner, Head of the Disney Corporation, is unequivocal: "To me, the pursuit of ideas is the only thing that matters," he has said, "You can always find capable people to do almost anything else."

For a company, successful innovation requires a conscious and explicit commitment and inevitably involves risk. It is best achieved in a "no blame" culture which recognizes that mistakes and failures are the natural and inevitable bedfellows of successful ideas. An innovative organization is typically characterized by informality, the free flow of information, little hierarchy or bureaucracy, and creative interaction within small cross-functional teams and small business units.

I mention the type of working environment that fosters innovative practices because this competency comes with a health warning for the Smart Careerist. The other fourteen competencies are more or less appropriate to display in just about any organization. But being innovative in an unsupportive environment, e.g. a risk-averse life assurance company, is difficult and occasionally downright dangerous.

Well, the pragmatists among us in those types of organization might be thinking, I'll just suppress my creative instincts, keep my head down for a bit, and then return to being my natural innovative self come the next change of company. Sadly, it may not be that easy. As you'll see in the next section, CVs these days are increasingly achievement-oriented and companies who prize innovation as much as Michael Eisner obviously does will be looking at your track record of coming up with and implementing new ideas.

Where you can't be blatantly innovative, i.e. and risk making the odd mistake, the trick is to take a more measured approach and implement only those ideas that you are confident will succeed. Come what may, and regardless of organizational culture, you will need that demonstrable record of achievement. Without it, you marketability will plummet. Unless, of course, you decide to approach only those organizations whose attitude to risk makes your current employer seem racy by comparison. A possible strategy perhaps, but not very "smart".

If a modicum of innovation *is* encouraged at the place where you now work, here are a few tips that will help to hone your capability in this area:

Listen to other people's views

Learn from their experience. Use their intuition and common sense as a source of new ideas. Encourage ideas from all around you. Benchmark other organizations.

Disagree constructively

Innovation depends on relentless self-questioning and the pursuit of continual improvement through constructive argument. Ongoing success is dependent on perpetual dissatisfaction with your performance.

Seek out new experiences

There are many ways to approach this one but here are just three tips on how to change your perspective:

1. Try a secondment to another part of the business.

2. Ask somebody who has just joined the organization what strikes them as odd about the place; a fresh pair of eyes will often highlight things that you have grown accustomed to and therefore no longer notice.

3. Go into newsagents, buy a handful of magazines outside of your immediate specialism, read what's going on in other fields and see if you can make any connections back to your working environment.

Join cross-functional teams whenever you get the chance

Most problems are best solved by interdisciplinary thinking, which successfully combines and applies different areas of expertise. Perhaps it's time to meet up with those people from production, finance, marketing and human resources (ah, the sacrifices we must make . . .).

Network

Knowledge is the only form of wealth that increases when you give it away. Share your ideas and see what comes back to you.

Be willing to allow events to change you

You have to be willing to grow. The prerequisites for growth are the openness to experience events and the willingness to be changed by them.

Capture accidents

The wrong answer is the right answer in search of a different question. Collect wrong answers as part of the process. Ask different questions.

Wait until the last minute

Let your mind drift. Explore tangents. Delay judgement. Postpone criticism.

Ask stupid questions

Growth is fuelled by desire and a degree of naivety, i.e. not knowing what can't be done. Assess the answer, not the question. Imagine learning throughout your life at the rate of an infant.

Shun precedent

Anybody who says "But we've always done it this way" shouldn't be allowed to hold up new ideas. If you can't convice them to come on board, work around them or, in the final analysis, move them out of your part of the business.

Think with your mind

Creativity is not device-dependent. Technology won't automatically help the creative process. Far better to take advantage of coffee breaks, cab rides, and other opportunities for a few minutes' downtime. Innovative ideas often come in places and at times that can surprise us.

GSOH

Laughter is a good barometer to measure how comfortably we are expressing ourselves. Show others that you have a good sense of humour.

SMART
PEOPLE
TO HAVE
ON YOUR
SIDE

Andy Law

Andy Law was the driving force behind the setting up of London-based advertising agency St Luke's and has been the company's iconoclastic chairman since 1995.

St Luke's is owned entirely by its employees. All physical resources – offices, desks, PCs, etc. – are shared, there is little hierarchy, and all employees are involved in almost all decisions, including setting their own pay rises. Rose the cleaner, one of 100 employees at the company, receives the same number of shares every year as Law himself.

In his book *Open Minds*, Law offers the following "Ten Ways to Create a Revolution in Your Company":

1. Ask yourself what you want out of life.
2. Ask yourself what really matters to you.
3. Give all your work-clothes to Oxfam and wear what you feel is really you.
4. Talk to people (even those you don't like) about 1 and 2. You should be feeling very uncomfortable now. You may even be sick. This is normal.
5. Give up something you most need at work (desk, company car, etc.).
6. Trust everyone you meet. Keep every agreement you make. You should be feeling a little better now.
7. Undergo a group experience (anything goes, parachuting, holidaying).
8. Rewrite your business plan to align all of the above with your customers.
9. Draw a line on the office floor and invite everyone to a brave new world.
10. Share everything you do and own fairly with everyone who crosses the line. You should be feeling liberated. Soon you will have, in this order, the following: grateful customers, inspired employees, friendly communities, money.

Continually challenge conventional wisdom, and question all the time. Ask yourself, "What does it mean?", "Why?", "What if?", and "How else could I do this?" For example, important questions are:

- Why does my organization exist?
- Why do we do things and have they any worthwhile purpose?
- What would we do differently if we started off again from scratch?
- Why don't we make the best use of our core competencies?
- Why don't we make it as easy as possible for our people to satisfy our customers?

Smart things to say about your career

The ten don'ts of innovation

1. Don't ditch your dreams – vision and imagination are vital.
2. Don't be afraid to stand out from the crowd – fly in the face of convention.
3. Don't hang about – one study concluded that profits fell by a third if a new product was six months late to market.
4. Don't think in black boxes – think interrelationships.
5. Don't forget reflection – the quiet times are the most creative.
6. Don't lose your curiosity – look, question and hypothesize.
7. Don't think in the past – look ahead and anticipate future customer requirements.
8. Don't put your head in the sand – learn by talking and listening to others.
9. Don't be bothered about rocking the boat – the comfort zone is no place for innovation.
10. Don't put the blinkers on – be open to new ideas.

Source: Philip Holden, *The Excellent Manager's Companion to Innovation* (Gower)

Smart things to know about your career

SMART VOICES

European law firm Olswang's e-commerce specialist John Esner has identified "an intolerance of failure" in the UK and Europe. "If you've been bankrupt in the US, it shows you're entrepreneurial and willing to take risks. Over here (bankruptcy) is seen as evidence of moral turpitude.

Financial Times, 8th February 2000

SMART QUOTES

Companies . . . need to build a forgiveness framework – a tolerance for error and failure – into their culture. A company that wants you to come up with a smart idea, implement that idea quickly, and learn in the process has to be willing to cut you some slack.

Jeffrey Pfeffer, Stanford Graduate School of Business, quoted in the *Fast Take* newsletter, 9 May 2000

13. LEADERSHIP

Managers and leaders – the difference

Managers: The word 'manager' is derived from the Latin *manus*, meaning 'hand'. The sixteenth-century Italian word *maneggiare* comes from this and was applied to the handling, training and control of horses. English soldiers subsequently brought the word back from Italy and applied it to the handling of armies and the control of ships. People who performed these vital jobs became known as 'managers'. Gradually, the word came into more general

use and was applied to anyone who had a responsibility for organizing activities and controlling their administration.

Leaders: The word 'leader' comes from laed, a word common to
all the old North European languages, meaning 'path', 'road',
'course of a ship at sea' or 'journey'. A leader therefore accompa-
nies people on a journey, guiding them to their destination. By
implication they hold people together as a group whilst leading
them in the right direction. A typical modern-day dictionary definition is one who rules, guides or inspires others.

David Turner, *Liberating Leadership* (1998)

*Smart Careerists know that success in their careers can often hang on
how effectively they motivate and unleash the potential of others. They
understand the Pygmalion effect, namely that people behave the way
they are treated: expect your team to fail and – sure enough – that's what
will happen; treat them as competent, talented individuals and they'll
live up to your expectations.*

*They also intuitively understand Buckminster Fuller's axiom that you
never change things by fighting the existing reality, that what you have to
do is build a new model that makes the existing model obsolete. In a
world of work where the rules of the game are being reshaped before our
eyes, their ability to put their own stamp on things enables them to
become masters of, and not victims of, circumstance.*

On the face of it, a business book by two Swedish professors about how
successful companies differ from their competitors doesn't sound like
the most riveting of reads. But *Funky Business* (ft.com, 2000) is no dry
theoretical tome; and authors Jonas Ridderstråle and Kjell Nordström
are not your standard issue academics – unless, that is, it's normal for
Swedish business professors to shave their heads, wear leather trousers,

describe themselves as funksters, and call their public appearances gigs rather than seminars.

Ridderstråle and Nordström are convinced that we are moving towards a world in which time and talent are the two critical commodities and it is how companies deal with these two factors that determines which who falls by the wayside and who moves through to the next round. The goal, and this is as good as it gets, is to be, as the authors put it, "momentarily ahead of the game".

In this world, leadership and management are more important than ever before. Gurus and commentators have been proclaiming this for years say Ridderstråle and Nordström, now it is reality:

> This is the age of time and talent, where we are selling, exploiting, organizing, hiring and packaging time and talent. The most critical resource wears shoes and walks out the door around five o'clock every day. As a result, management and leadership are keys to competitive advantage. They differentiate you from the mass. How you attract, retain and motivate your people is more important than technology; how you treat your customers and suppliers, more important than technology. How a company is managed and how a company is

SMART
PEOPLE
TO HAVE
ON YOUR
SIDE

Richard Pascale

For twenty years, Richard Pascale was on the faculty of the Stanford Business School. He is now an Associate Fellow of Oxford University. He is a consultant and a writer. His third book, *Surfing the Edge of Chaos*, was published in 2000.

The following key points are adapted from a letter by Pascale that appeared in the *Harvard Business Review* (May–June 1997). He wrote in response to an article by Ronald Heifetz and Donald Laurie on leadership published in the January–February 1997 issue.

- Leadership occurs only when those in responsible roles consciously endeavour to make happen what wouldn't happen anyway. Heifetz and Laurie call this adaptive work, and it always occurs outside one's comfort zone. Adaptive work is in contrast to technical work, in which executives draw upon a repertoire of pre-existing solutions to address the problems at hand. Technical work is nothing to be ashamed of but it does not require leadership.

- At face value, the distinction between technical work and adaptive work is not difficult to comprehend. The trouble is, with "leadership" being so fashionable these days, many executives don't like to think that they are merely making happen what was going to happen anyway. The idea that most people who occupy executive positions are merely stewards of the inevitable is provocative.

- The authors' second radical idea is to divorce leadership from personality traits. Charisma, boldness, even the capacity to generate organizational purpose are absent from their model. Instead, the central theme shining through their work is mindfulness. They highlight the capacity to discern when traditional solutions are not likely to produce the desired results. That discernment must be followed not by the exercise of personality traits

When a team from McKinsey set out to discover why some companies were able to move to higher performance levels while others failed, their research came to a surprising conclusion. The make-or-break factor is not top management but a new breed in the middle of organizations – real change leaders (RCLs), who become a critical lynchpin between customers, employees and senior management. And what exactly characterizes an RCL?

This is how Jon Katzenbach, who wrote up the team's findings in a book called *Real Change Leaders* (Nicholas Brealey, 1997), characterized it:

The best RCLs develop a unique combination of skills, values, attributes, and attitudes for a wide variety of change and performance situations. They are able to meet increasingly demanding standards for better and better performance results. But they do it by capitalizing on the hidden potential of their people, and without sacrificing the longer-term quality and service requirements in their markets. They also demonstrate an unusual ability to apply different leadership approaches when and as the circumstances require it. They have learned how to obtain better people-results as well as better performance-results. Last but not least, they seem to be motivated more by making a difference than by climbing up through the hierarchy.

When these new-breed change leaders rise to meet more demanding change challenges, they face a never ending task of maintaining the optimum balance between faster and better results, and more mass and momentum of people. As this flexible new breed emerges, the old-style, uni-dimensional middle managers will increasingly end up like the bitter cowboys of the past. Paradoxically, except for their attitudes and mindsets, many could master the skills and develop the flexibility and agility of the change leaders who are beginning to replace them.

Part of a growing backlash against the 1990's obsession with stripping out layers of middle management, this highly readable book aims to show senior managers how to create and tap into this newly rehabilitated source of leadership capability.

led are vital differentiators. They can create sustainable uniqueness. But at the same time as management and leadership have reached maturity as potent competitive weapons, their very nature has changed.

The boss is dead. No longer can we believe in a leader who claims to know more about everything and who is always right. Management by numbers is history. Management by

Smart things to say about your career

fear won't work. If management is people, management must become hu-management.

The job is dead. No longer can we believe in having a piece of paper saying job description at the top. The new realities call for far greater flexibility. Throughout most of the twentieth century, managers averaged one job and one career. Now, we are talking about two careers and seven jobs. The days of the long-serving corporate man, safe and sound in the dusty recesses of the corporation, are long gone. Soon the emphasis will be on getting a life instead of a career, and work will be viewed as a series of gigs or projects.

Inevitably, new roles demand new skills. Thirty years ago, we had to learn one new skill per year. Now, it is one new skill per day. Tomorrow, it may be one new skill per hour.

14. DEVELOP YOUR BRAND

You may have heard the Woody Allen line that 90% of success at work is about turning up. Perhaps that was true a while back when applied to the type of person who started at the bottom of the organizational pile and liked it there. These days, that attitude won't even achieve survival, let alone success.

If "just turning up" is a no-brain strategy, the Smart Careerist knows that "just being good at what you do" is not that much better. Over 2000 years ago, the classical historian Sallust wrote of Cato that he "preferred to be rather than to seem good". In the 21st century workplace, you need both – what Tom Peters calls the "steak and the sizzle".

You must have come across them – those selfless, unassuming, committed and dedicated individuals who exist in varying numbers in just about every company. You know the ones I mean: they concentrate on doing the best possible job they can, claiming no credit and paying no real heed to ensuring that their contribution is acknowledged by the company.

At one level, there is something admirable about them. But as somebody who spends quite a bit of his time counselling people who have been made redundant, I know how often it is these self-effacing, highly capable and loyal employees who are the first to be "let go" by their organizations. If nobody knows how good you really are, what would your company expect to miss if you weren't around any more?

For the Smart Careerist, ensuring that your contribution is recognized and valued is a crucial plank in the game plan. But how best to achieve this?

SMART
ANSWERS
TO TOUGH
QUESTIONS

Enter Tom Peters, co-author of *In Search of Excellence* and probably the world's best-known management guru. In recent years, Peters has been looking at how changes at a corporate, national and global level impact on the nature of work for us as individuals. It is a topical theme that takes a variety of guises – knowledge workers making a living out of Charles Leadbeater's "thin air"; McKinsey warning its clients that the biggest challenge for companies is "the war for talent"; Charles Handy's "portfolio workers"; Harriet Rubin's "soloists"; business magazines like *Fast Company* devoted to Me Inc. or me.com and full of advice on "why it pays to quit", how you should be hotdesking with colleagues, telecommuting from home, and generally reconsidering your whole future.

In August 1997, Peters contributed an article to *Fast Company* magazine titled "The Brand Called You: You Can't Move Up If You Don't Stand Out". In it, he argues that "regardless of age, regardless of position, regardless of the business we happen to be in, all of us need to understand the importance of branding. We are CEOs of our own companies:

KILLER QUESTIONS

To help you define your brand, ask yourself: What do I want to be famous for?

Me Inc. To be in business today, our most important job is to be head marketer for the brand called You."

The article (which, by the way, can be found on *Fast Company*'s excellent website at www.fastcompany.com/online/10/brandyou.html) is a brilliant synthesis of economic, marketing and business themes. It ends with a stark conclusion:

It's this simple: you are a brand. You are in charge of your brand. There is no single path to success. And there is no one right way to create the brand called You. Except this: Start today. Or else.

SMART QUOTES

You're every bit as much a brand as Nike, Coke, Pepsi or the Body Shop. To start thinking like your own favourite brand manager, ask yourself the same question the brand managers at Nike, Coke, Pepsi or the Body Shop ask themselves: What is it that my product or service does that makes it different? Give yourself the traditional 15-words-or-less contest challenge. Take the time to write down your answer. And then take the time to read it. Several times.

If your answer wouldn't light up the eyes of a prospective client or command a vote of confidence from a satisfied past client, or – worst of all – if it doesn't grab you, then you've got a big problem. It's time to give some serious thought and even more serious effort to imagining and developing yourself as a brand.

Start by identifying the qualities or characteristics that make you distinctive from your competitors – or your colleagues. What have you done lately – this week – to make yourself stand out? What would your colleagues or your customers say is your greatest and clearest strength? Your most noteworthy (as in, worthy of note) personal trait?

Tom Peters, in his article titled 'The Brand Called You: You Can't Move Up If You Don't Stand Out', *Fast Company* August 1997

Two years later Peters expanded the article into book form with *Brand You 50*. The book consists of, in his words, "fifty ways to transform yourself from an employee into a brand that shouts distinction, commitment and passion". Stripped to their essence, the 50 ways more or less boil down three key ideas – one, decide what you want to do; two, then do it obsessively; and three, pay more attention to how you present yourself to the world.

Five ways to build your profile

1. Find a mentor: Time was when mentors used to pick their protégés, these days protégés are likely to be picking their mentors.

2. Look the part: Dress in a style that suits your job, and which matches peoples expectations.

3. Become an active member of your professional association. It will increase your professional know-how and help you build an impressive set of contacts.

4. Specialize: Be the person that everybody turns to when the budget needs checking, or the computer goes wrong, or when people want a good listener.

5. Develop your presentation skills.

Six ways to undermine your profile

1. Dressing inconsistently.

2. Dressing beneath you.

3. Allowing others to interrupt when you are expressing yourself well.

4. Appearing nervous, anxious, or indecisive.

5. Not joining a professional association, or not reading your professional journal.

6. Projecting a can't do or negative attitude.

Smart things to say about your career

15. MAKING IT HAPPEN

You have between 30 and 60 days to make an impression as the new leader, to convince everyone that you're the right person, and to show people that you're doing something. To make a difference, you have one year.
Nina Disesa, Chairman and Chief Creative Officer,
McCann-Erickson

Most people say they're too busy . . . but we all have at least 15 minutes a days. If you use that time well, 15 minutes can matter.
Danny Seo, Heaven on Earth: 15-minute Miracles to
Change the World (Pocket Books, 1999)

A friend of mine has a favourite four-letter acronym – JFDI – which, in the Parental Guidance version, stands for Just Flipping-well Do It. "Making it happen" is about the desire to get on and take action, and to do it to a high standard.

For the Smart Careerist, this is the point where the rubber hits the road. The other fourteen competencies count for little if not accompanied by the drive to achieve something.

With the publication of *In Search of Excellence* in 1982, Tom Peters and co-author Bob Waterman changed the way organizations thought about themselves. Notions of embracing a paradoxical world of constant change, of providing exemplary customer service and of the need for high-speed response are now mainstream corporate thinking, but during the mid-1980s, the challenge laid down by Peters and Waterman was enormous.

In their book, they identified eight characteristics of excellent companies. Although they subsequently acknowledged that their recipe was incomplete, many of the individual elements remain valid. In particular their view that management is about taking action – two of their eight characteristics are bias to action and hands-on management – and getting things done still hold good.

Here are eight examples of the things that *Smart Careerist* with a high bias to action do:

1. Take risks – go for results.

2. Treat failure as an opportunity for positive change.

3. Initiate, innovate – don't wait for things to come to them.

4. Persist in the face of obstacles and difficulties.

5. Make connections – network.

6. Keep a record of all their achievements.

7. Support and praise others when they deserve it.

8. Make the most of themselves physically.

Enough already – it's time to get on.

Sometimes it's easier to determine what to do when you have somebody who can help you think things through. A marketing company chief who signed up to a mentoring service four years ago has benefited from overhauling his approach to business. He introduced a policy of openness, making all business information available to staff. He also introduced flexi-time and improved holiday entitlements. As a result he created greater staff loyalty and improved productivity.

THE SMART CAREERIST COMPETENCY SET – A FEW FINAL THOUGHTS

The rewards of ageing always seem to slightly outweigh the freshness of youth.
> Douglas Coupland, novelist, *Observer*, 27 February 2000

Traveler, our time together has begun a graceful yet irreversible learning process. I have given you these laws not to bind you, but to free you.
> Dan Millman

Fifteen competencies are a lot to get to grips with. As I mentioned at the outset of this section, though, these 15 don't represent the whole gamut of skills and capabilities that the Smart Careerist needs.

Here are five more competencies that were "bubbling under" the top 15 (although, depending on the circumstances, any of these could displace one of the featured competencies in importance):

How to ask for a payrise

- Be positive: don't be apologetic

- Be prepared: put together your case based on your achievements and your commitment to the company. Don't say why you need the money: it's your problem, not your company's, that your last car service cost so much. Negotiate – know what you would like and what you would settle for

- Get your timing right: don't catch your boss on the hoof and make a pitch. Make an appointment; go for the time of day that might catch your boss at their most mellow. Mot fifteen minutes before they are due to meet with the MD. And if on the morning of the meeting the company has announced a dip in profits or that it is about to lay off 20 % of the workforce, cancel the appointment.

- Don't issue an ultimatum or threaten to resign unless you're prepared to go through with it.

Smart things to say about your career

SMART QUOTES

We don't automatically admire quick thinking – it can mean glibness and superficiality, we may have noticed. But we do associate it with intelligence, these days more than ever. Lightning calculators must surely be smart, the occasional idiot savant notwithstanding. Quick-witted people, the mentally agile, those who can think on their feet – we may not always choose them to be captain or president, but we tend to respect them. We have heard of unhurried qualities like wisdom and sagacity, but we think nonetheless that the students who plod through laborious calculations cannot be quite as smart as their comrades who snap their fingers and know the answer. Some modern businesses have built this assumption into their hiring procedures. . . . Some companies, such as Microsoft, are particularly known for hiring on this basis of mind-speed and for peppering job applicants with SAT-like questions in interviews so as to bring the quality into sharp relief. Much of life has become a game show, our fingers perpetually poised above the buzzer. We're either the quick or the dead. To be quick it used to be enough merely to be alive. Now we expect repartee and fast response times too.

James Gleick, *Faster* (Little Brown, 1999)

16. BE OPPORTUNISTIC

- Don't wait to be asked.

- Volunteer to edit the newsletter or organize the Christmas party.

- Offer yourself to go on that senior management programme that your boss is too busy (too disorganized more like) to make.

- If the MD gets into your lift, make sure you say something.

- Get yourself onto project teams.

17. BE POLITICALLY ASTUTE

- Be aware of who are the "risers" and "fallers" in the top management team.

- Don't be openly critical of senior management actions – asking an awkward question at the Employee AGM might help you become the people's choice but you are unlikely to endear yourself to the powers that be.

- Look for the message under the message.

- Read Machiavelli's *The Prince*.

I have some unease about featuring this as a competency but I've been lobbied persuasively by a few people who would maintain that many a career has foundered on a single politically inept act. It seems to me though that if you're to be judged by your political nous rather than your many other capabilities, then you are probably working for the wrong company.

18. EMBRACE THE TECHNOLOGY

Research by GlobalChange.com, a management trends consultancy that specializes in the digital economy, shows that fewer than half of Britain's senior directors can send and receive their own e-mails and 60% are unable to log on to their company's website without help. There may be something faintly comical and endearing about the greybeards struggling to find the on/off switch. However, if you're a thirty- or fortysomething with a disdain for new technology, be warned: there's a generation of internet-savvy, technologically-hip people coming through who may well turn out to be the reason you don't get your next promotion.

19. COMMIT TO LIFE-LONG LEARNING

- Recognize that the skills, knowledge and experience that got you where you are today won't be enough to get you where you want to be in the future.

- "Learning" does not always have to equal "courses". Read a book; talk to an expert; surf the net for information; just practice; take a secondment to another part of the business; go and do some work in the community;

20. BE A FLUENT COMMUNICATOR, BOTH VERBALLY AND IN WRITING:

- Feel confident that you can give a prepared talk that has style, substance and clarity.

- Aim to be 'media-friendly' at all times. It's now pretty much impossible for a politician to succeed without being a skilled communicator. People who are capable at their work but who don't come across well on TV or in person will struggle to move into senior roles in the future.

- To polish your writing skills, try reading *The Pyramid Principle* by Barbara Minto (Pitman, 1991), the best book around on how to present complex ideas in writing.

- Work and re-work your CV – it's your career calling card.

Interlude 2

The New Language of Work

The accidental career: This is what you have if your career has evolved by chance circumstances rather than through positive choice.

Blamestorming: Sitting around in a group discussing who was responsible for a deadline being missed or a project failing.

Career choke: This is what happens to your career when you don't get that job - say when your boss moves on - that you fondly imagined was yours

Chumming: The indiscriminate distribution of one's business card in the hope of attracting the interest of somebody important.

Clusters: Critical masses in one place of linked industries that enjoy a high level of success in their particular field. Famous examples are Silicon Valley and Hollywood but clusters can be found everywhere.

Counselling out: A new strategy for getting rid of unwanted staff has been christened. If people are not performing, they are helped to see that it's time to look for jobs elsewhere.

Creepback: A tendency for former staff to be re-hired on the quiet after over-enthusiastic sackings have been made.

Desk rage: Long hours and the growing pressures of the workplace are leading to increasing outbreaks of office strife. As stress builds in the office, workers are increasingly venting their frustrations on colleagues.

Downshifting: The deliberate decision to simplify and enrich your life (by balancing work and home life, reducing levels of financial commitment) at the expense of your income

E-lancers: independent contractors connected through personal computers and electronic networks. These electronically connected freelancers – e-lancers – join together into fluid and temporary networks to produce and sell goods and services.

Head-shunting: A term that describes when employers suggest to head-hunters that they should contact a capable but troublesome employee. Companies occasionally pay a discreet fee to the headhunter, reckoning that to be cheaper than the cost of an exit package or an industrial tribunal.

The Internot: Business executives or organisations that see no value from getting online.

Micro-careers: With the death of the job for life went the notion of getting paid to do broadly the same thing throughout your working days.

Micro-careers are those distinct and separate chunks of activity that will characterise an individual's working life in the 21st century.

Out of the garage: A term for a young company that has just moved to its first real office.

PYMWYMIC: A company that acts according to its values and beliefs, as in a Put Your Money Where Your Mouth Is Company

SOHO: Small Office, Home Office – a term used to describe what in North America is currently the fastest growing category of employment, namely the rise of self-employment and home-based businesses.

The third wardrobe: A term used to denote smart casual clothing that is replacing traditional business-wear.

4

Moving On

According to Fish4.co.uk, a fifth of workers in the UK made a New Year's resolution to look for new jobs.

Guardian, 6 January 2001

"Should I Stay or Should I Go?"

Title of a song by The Clash

The Smart Careerist knows it makes sense to review on a regular basis, say every six months or so, the state of their career. There are nine main choices on the table for consideration at these reviews, namely:

1. **Continue as you are:** There is no inherent merit in chopping and changing every six months. Pursuing that kind of thinking *ad absurdum* would mean around 80 different "packets of works" in a 40-year career. The key question is whether staying positively enhances your career prospects. If you are going to be learning nothing new, then the value of your career stock will stay static at best.

2. **New role in the same organization:** Internal career development can be an excellent way of moving into new fields, and learning new skills. Because you would be staying in your current organization, you would not have the distraction of having to absorb a new culture or a different set of operating principles. You would also know who's who. If you are unhappy in the discipline in which you currently work, this can be a good way to find another area that might suit you better.

3. **Similar role in a new organization:** This is perhaps the easiest proposition to take to the external job marketplace. When assessing who they want to join their company, employers tend to be pretty conservative. If they're looking for a Finance Director, and you're already the FD of a similar enterprise, you're much more likely to succeed than a Finance Manager from a completely different sector who is looking for a promotion.

4. **New role in a new organization:** After the easiest proposition to take to the external job marketplace, we come to the hardest. It is possible to change career direction and companies at the same time, but you need to work hard at it and be very convincing and persuasive about (a) why you're trying to make the move and (b) your ability to perform the new role effectively.

5. **Retrain and go for a radical change:** The trainer who became an ordained priest. The accountant who went into teaching. The bank clerk who became an aromatherapist. I've known people who have made each of these moves. It takes real commitment and a sizeable dollop of courage to abandon one career to pursue another (although in each of these three cases, the people concerned main-

tained that what they did was the only common-sense option open to them).

6. **Start your own business:** There are two unusual facets to starting your own business. The first is that you do not normally have to go through a selection process – you decide whether to give yourself a job. The second facet is that you decide what type of business it is and what market you will be selling to.

7. **Go for a portfolio of roles and activities:** This involves turning your hand to a variety of activities at the same time. Management guru Charles Handy coined the term "portfolio working" to describe people who spend their time in any permutation of one or more of the following: paid work, unpaid work, study and learning, and housework.

8. **Pave the way:** Sometimes it can make more sense to actively plan for the next move rather than to try to make it right now. Spending time on things like getting your professional qualification upgraded, learning a new software package, researching the market place, broadening your experience with an internal secondment, and so on might be the most positive way of heading toward the job you want next.

9. **Positively embrace early retirement:** Not much to say about this one. A perfectly legit option if you can afford it, but I'd be surprised that you're reading this book if this is something to which you are giving serious thought.

Changing jobs

> Successful job hunting is a learned skill. You have to study it. You have to prac-
> tice it. You have to master it, just like any new skill. And master it thoroughly
> because you'll need it all the rest of your life.
>
> Richard Bolles, What Color Is Your Parachute?

When the time comes for you to move on from your current employer,
there are four main methods by which you are likely to locate your next
role.

• Networking

• Responding to an advertisement

• Going via agencies and headhunters

• Approaching companies speculatively

Of these, networking accounts for most job moves, and not just at the
more senior end of the market. The 15-year-old who uses one of his
friends who has a paper round to check out with the newsagent whether
there are any vacancies is networking just as much as two MDs on a golf
course.

As to the other three methods, they all have at their heart two key elements, namely:

1. Presenting yourself in writing; and

2. Meeting people in person

In the job-hunting process, the normal vehicles by which these happen are (a) the CV/application form and (b) the job interview. Let's look at each in turn.

Preparing to write a CV

If you don't have a CV or it has been some years since you last updated your CV, the first step in the process is to spend some time gathering together information. If you spent time on some of the early exercises in Chapter 2 "Taking Stock", you'll already have a lot of information to hand

Make chronological lists of your work experience, education, and training. In particular, jot down any achievements that might impress a potential employer. Quantify them as much as you can. Some examples of the type of information to note:

- Size of budgets you were responsible for

- Money you've saved the organization

- Number of people managed

- Improvements you've achieved in turn-around times, customer satisfaction, and sales turnover

Writing a CV

Here are five principles to bear in mind when putting together a CV:

1. Keep it simple

2. Keep it short

3. Make it look good

4. Be positive

5. Customize your CV to each job applied for

1. Keep it simple

You want to be absolutely certain that the reader will understand every point you make. Before you send it off, check through the CV for:

- *"Company speak":* have you used terminology that people outside your present company might struggle to understand. This can be more difficult than it sounds, particularly when you have worked somewhere for a few years and you may have absorbed the company dialect by some form of corporate osmosis. If in doubt, try showing your CV to a neutral third party.

- *Jargon and acronyms:* as with "company speak", these are to be avoided if possible and only used at all if you are convinced that the reader will understand.

- *Typing errors:* OK, sounds obvious I know, but it is *so* easy to let a few slip through. There's a psychological trait that can lead us to see on the page what we expect to see rather than what was actually written. If you can, ask somebody to look through your CV for typos. Don't rely on your software package's spellchecker – the number of senior "mangers" that show up on CVs is staggering.

2. Keep it short

As far as possible, stick to two sides of A4. CVs are subject to the whims of changing taste, and just now long and detailed CVs are definitely out of fashion. Besides, keeping it short disciplines the writer to be concise and relevant.

3. Make it look good

- The CV should be typed of course. A hand-written version might show that you're a quirky individualist, but just as an American friend of mine defines a pedestrian as "somebody who has parked their car", so most recruiters regard a candidate who sends in a hand-written CV as somebody who either can't use or can't be bothered to gain access to a computer. Neither of these will endear a candidate to a company.

- Use quality paper, typically white, as it photocopies the best. There are those who swear by using tinted paper in the belief that this helps their CV catch the eye. Most recruiters swear with equal force that it doesn't make a blind bit of difference.

- Keep it uncluttered. Use lots of white space (handy for the recruiter to make notes on).

- Avoid using lots of different fonts – it just looks messy. Go for one font that is clear, distinct and easy-on-the-eye – **Arial**, Times Roman, or **Gill Sans**, for example.

- Use bullet points, bold type, spacing, etc., to make the CV look as attractive and readable as possible.

KILLER
QUESTIONS

Here are four key questions you need to ask yourself every time you consider going for a job in another company:

- What do I offer?
- What does the organization in question want?
- What do I want?
- What does the organization in question offer?

4. Be positive

- Only include details that positively sell you. Your CV is a marketing document, not a confession.

- When it comes to describing your knowledge and experience, don't put in information simply because you feel it ought to go in. Ask yourself the question: Does this fact make it more likely that I'll be called for interview? If it does, in it goes.

But a word of warning: *don't fabricate evidence.* And not just because there's a chance you'll be found out (although with more and more companies using CV-checking services, this likelihood is steadily growing). I know it is sometimes tempting to make yourself even more irresistible to a potential employer by augmenting reality with a few fictional excesses. Don't do it – the truth is liable to out at some point, leaving you facing anything from embarrassment and rejection through to dismissal. Besides that, one lie undermines the credibility of all your genuine accomplishments.

5. Customize your CV to each job applied for

Perhaps the most crucial point of all. These days, a CV is not just a marketing document but a one-to-one marketing document. Sir Arthur Conan Doyle's creation Sherlock Holmes once said "The highest importance in the art of detection is to be able to recognize out of a number of facts which are incidental and which are vital." This is also of "the highest importance" when it comes to writing a CV. Show specifically how your experience matches the company's needs: if their advertisement asks for somebody who has worked with younger staff, and you've had experience of introducing three trainees into the department who have all gone on the be offered permanent positions, make sure that you tell them.

Look out for signals in the advertisement about what they are expecting of candidates. In March 2001, a county council was seeking applicants for a PR post that would involve promoting bus transport, but a company car was being offered with the job. A spokesman for the council was quoted as hoping that the person appointed would demonstrate personal commitment to the job by not taking up the car offer. Now there's a clue about one way to impress/not impress the council!

KILLER
QUESTIONS

- What makes you special?
- A Unique Selling Point is what makes you stand out from the crowd. What particular combination of skills and experience might give you an advantage over others going for the same job?

What doesn't go into your CV

1. Salary: don't mention what you're currently earning unless you're specifically asked to. Better to include salary details in a covering letter if necessary.

2. References: not necessary at this stage.

3. Weaknesses: this is a marketing document, so stress the positive not the negative

4. Unnecessary headings: there's no need to put 'Curriculum Vitae' at the top of your CV. Besides being a statement of the bleeding obvious, it takes up valuable space that you could devote to making a selling point.

5. Clichés: there's a temptation to sprinkle phrases like "proactive",

"self-starting team-player", "key player", "leader of men", "proven man manager".

6. Don't use acronyms and abbreviations unless you're absolutely confident that the reader will recognize them.

Sometimes, your first approach to a company is by telephone rather than in writing. Whether you're ringing up to enquire whether there are any vacancies, to find out a bit more about a job, or simply to request an application form, the crucial point to remember about telephone cold calling is that it's the company that is "cold", not you. Don't forget to research companies before contacting.

- When you make the call, be confident and professional. To help with this, use cue cards to help you script out the call so that those important early seconds of the conversation run smoothly.

- Keep positive. The last thing you want is a conversation that goes along the lines of "Hello, you don't know me, actually I'm not really sure who you are, I daresay you would rather be doing something else. Look I'll go. I am the weakest link. Goodbye."

- Introduce yourself to them and explain why you're calling

- Be prepared, if asked, to give a brief summary of your main skills and experience. Sell your skills and achievements. The accent here is on relevance: replaying your triumph in the county table tennis championships of 1982 is not the way to maintain the attention of the decision-maker.

- Be sensitive to the mood of the person you're talking to. If their cat threw up on the new sofa that morning, the washing machine leaked, somebody drove into the back of them on the way into work, they lost a filling, and their star performer just handed in their notice, chances are your telephone call is not going to catch them in the heartiest of good humour.

- End by confirming the next step, ideally a meeting

- Keep a list of the phone calls made with dates and details of what happened.

7. If you are unemployed or have been made redundant, don't mention this in your initial approach. There's no need at this stage to say why you're in the job market.

Different types of CV

There are three main types of CV

- Chronological

- Functional

- Achievement

Chronological

This type of CV details your education and the jobs you have held in sequence. The most effective use of a chronological CV is to list your experience in reverse chronology, i.e. starting with the current or most recent role first and then moving back in time, and then going on to do the same with your education.

A typical layout is as follows:

Section 1:   Contact details (name, address, contact number, email)

Section 2:   Profile statement (see the section below on Profiles)

Section 3:   Employment history

Section 4:   Education and training/professional qualifications

Section 5:   Interests (try to give examples that indicate positive qualities like leadership, personal fitness, intellectual capability,
etc.)

Section 6:   Personal information (age, marital status, children and
so on – optional whether to include this information,
although recruiters seem to prefer to have these details

The main benefit of a chronological layout is that the first page of your
CV features prominently your most recent (and typically most senior)
role. Since you only have seconds to grab the attention of the person
reading your CV, you want you make sure that you get all your big-hit-
ting points over early.

Q: What if I don't have everything that the advertisement asks for?

A: It's often the case that people don't have absolutely every qualification or
piece of experience mentioned in the advertisement. Try to determine what are
the "must-haves" for the job. These are not necessarily what the advert
describes as essential; "Must have a good working knowledge of Sage
accounting software" might well mean in reality "If you know a different piece of
accounting software, we'd be prepared to pay for some Sage training to bring
you up to speed"; "Must have a degree" is often not as fixed a requirement as
it sounds. As a rough guideline, if you can match 60% of the stated requirements, it can be worth going for. After all, you have nothing to lose but the
price of a stamp.

SMART
ANSWERS
TO TOUGH
QUESTIONS

The drawbacks are that:

• If you're a bit of a job-hopper, this type of CV displays that very
graphically

- Any gaps in your history are likely to stand out

- Your skills and achievements may not be signalled clearly to the reader if they are spread over all the roles you have held

- If your most recent role does not embody the career direction you are looking to pursue, it may cast a cloud of doubt in the mind of the reader

That said, the chronological CV is still far and away the most widely used format for presenting career history. Most recruitment managers still have a preference to see a candidate's information in this format.

Functional

This type of CV is organized by skill rather than job titles. It largely ignores chronology and puts the focus instead on the skills and abilities that the individual has that are relevant to the role applied for. Examples of areas that might be relevant are leadership, project management, customer service, and so on.

The main drawbacks are they are more time-consuming to draw up and that they are sometimes regarded with a degree of suspicion by people more used to seeing "traditional" chronological CVs.

Nonetheless, this type of CV can be productive when most recent career history is not particularly indicative of future direction.

Achievement

An achievement-based CV focuses on specific examples of where people have made a positive difference in the roles they have held. The focus is less on the nitty-gritty of somebody's job responsibilities and more on their personal impact.

Q: Which type of CV is currently in fashion?

A: The best CV to use will vary according to circumstances, but a chronological CV that also gives some examples of achievements in each role will take some beating.

SMART ANSWERS TO TOUGH QUESTIONS

Profiles

A profile statement is your opportunity to distill your proposition down to a few well-chosen words (typically around three or four lines' worth). It gives a concise overview of relevant skills, experience, and qualifications. At their best, profiles are like a good advertisement – snappy, focused, and enticing. At their worst, they reek of self-congratulatory bullshit.

A profile statement is an optional part of the CV, but most professionals in the recruitment field recommend them.

Application forms

Much loved still by local government, public services, and many of the denationalized industries. Much disliked by most jobhunters. Ask any recruitment manager and they will tell you that asking people to complete an application form cuts down the number of applicants for a position.

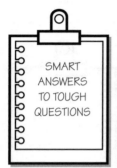

Q: Is it a good idea to pay somebody else to produce my CV?

A: It can be tempting to hand responsibility over to a professional CV writer.

On the face of it, they are familiar with the latest tricks and techniques, and can make sure that your CV looks contemporary.

On the negative side:

- They won't necessarily understand the terminology specific to your particular line of work, and therefore might misrepresent your experience.
- CVs produced by third parties may not convey the real you.
- They can look like a production line job, rather than the product of your own efforts. (I have an HR friend who swears that he can spot not only whether somebody has had help with putting their CV together but also which company or agency provided the assistance.)

There may be value in getting a first draft of your CV produced by a professional agency, particularly if you're suffering from CV writer's block or just don't find it easy to express yourself in writing. However, you will still need to tweak the CV every time it goes out to make sure that you emphasize the points relevant to the position you're going after.

Since from a recruiter's perspective, advertisements are more likely to attract too many rather than too few applications, the use of application forms can be a nifty way of reducing company time and money. This means that if you can face the prospect of completing an application form without the will to live totally deserting you, you'll find that you will typically be up against a smaller field of competition.

Other reasons that companies like application forms:

- Application forms ask all candidates for the same information, and are regarded by the Advisory, Conciliation and Arbitration Service *et al.* as good equal-opportunities practice.

- They allow the company to specify the information that applicants need to provide.

- They allow a readier comparison between candidates.

Completing an application form

- For most of us, it's worthwhile taking a photocopy of the form so that we can draft out a rough version first. Multiple crossings out, and your handwriting getting smaller as you try ever more desperately to squeeze your doubtless brilliant prose into a tiny space on the form, are great ways to demonstrate that you're as human as the rest of us but they don't go down a bundle with the overworked soul in the personnel department who has to wade through dozens of forms besides yours.

- Neatness counts. Use a black pen ideally – light turquoise ink may demonstrate what an individualistic, creative person you are but it's a bugger to read and even worse to photocopy.

- Complete the form fully. Tempting though it might be to send a CV instead and write "See my CV" in some sections of the form, you'll be labelled lazy and disinterested.

- Ask yourself what are they really looking? Answer this and you can begin to tailor your response. If you're given space to make a personal statement about yourself, use it. Most people would say that this is their least favourite part of an application form, but it is a major opportunity to distinguish yourself from the competition. Highlight some relevant achievements; demonstrate that you've taken the time to find out something about the company ("Given your recently announced plans to expand into Europe . . .").

Electronic CVs

Smart things to say about your career

If you don't know already, find out on which day of the week jobs in your subject area are advertised in the different national newspapers.

There are estimates that anything up to 80% of medium-to-large sized employers are now using some form of electronic scanning to help them process CVs. Even smaller companies are buying in recruitment services from external agencies that use scanning systems.

Growing numbers of recruiters now use electronic CV databases to search for people with specific experience and qualifications.

How does this work?

On arrival, a CV is fed through a scanner and then converted into a "readable" file. The computer then searches the file for keywords (i.e. relevant skills, experience, knowledge, abilities, and education) and places the CV in an appropriate database. When a vacancy comes up, the employer uses an applicant tracking system to locate and extract those CVs that contain the keywords associated with the role being filled. It's best to describe your experience with concrete words rather than vague descriptions. You can increase your list of keywords by including specifics, e.g. list the names of software you use, such as Microsoft Word and Lotus 1-2-3.

It's a lot easier to match people with "hard" skills than people with "soft" skills, and so the individuals who are popular on databases are people in professions like engineering, computer science, finance, accounting, marketing, management, and human resources. On the other hand, people working in "softer" areas like fashion design or the visual arts may find that their experience does not suit this medium.

Forrester Research expects the worldwide market for online recruitment to be worth more than $7bn by 2005. It generated $1.1bn in revenues last year. Recruitment is one of five Internet sectors that remain very profitable.

Sunday Telegraph, 18 March 2001

To help your CV go through a scanner as painlessly as possible, try the following:

- Use white A4 paper, printed on one side only

- Provide a laser-printed original if possible. A typewritten original or a high quality photocopy is OK. Avoid dot-matrix printouts and low-quality copies.

- Do not fold or staple.

- Use standard typefaces and avoid fancy treatments such as italics, underline, shadows and reverses (white letters on black background).

- Use a font size of 10–14 points.

- Use boldface and/or all capital letters for section headings (but don't confuse the OCR software by using a typeface where the letters touch each other.

- Don't go for anything gimmicky – two column format, a CV that looks like newspapers or newsletters.

Q: Does it matter that I've just been made redundant?

A: There's a myth that "it's easier to get a job from a job", in other words, that employers are better disposed to applicants with jobs, and that you're damaged goods if you are on the market due to redundancy.

Not true. Statistically, there's no evidence to back this up.

Redundancy isn't what it was. With around five million redundanices in the UK over the past five years, it has become a commonplace occurrence. The vast majority of redundancies occur on the back of a downturn in business, mergers, or restructuring within a business. Against this backdrop, most people who are made redundant are simply in the wrong role at the wrong time.

Most recruiters pay little heed to it these days when assessing the suitability of a candidate. In fact, there are some recruiters who regard it as a positive advantage because it means that the individual is definitely in play and also likely to be available at short notice.

By the way, if you can secure some outplacement support as part of your leaving package, grab it. It's particularly helpful if it's been a few years since you were last active in the external job market. There are some excellent providers in the outplacement market – Coutts, DBM, Penna Sanders and Sidney, to name three of the biggest. Typically, they'll help you think through what needs to go into a CV, critique your early drafts, give you some interview practice, and generally help you tune up for the marketplace.

Covering letters

There are two schools of thought among recruiters about covering letters: there are those who read every word avidly because they see the covering letter as the candidate's chance to set out their particular claim to be seriously considered for a role; and there are those who will automatically toss them in the bin without reading them.

Unfortunately, and I say "unfortunately" because crafting a decent letter is a time-consuming business, it probably makes sense to act on the assumption that the recruiter is interested in reading a covering letter even if they're not.

Covering letters can usefully be broken down into three sections:

1. Establish the connection

2. Make the pitch

3. Where to from here

1. **Establish the connection:** Why are you writing at this particular time? Is it in response to an advertisement, in which case say so and identify where you saw the ad (this can help recruiters to identify which papers or magazines bring in the best response). If the approach is more speculative on your part, still try to give a reason why you're interested in that particular company. A covering letter which looks like it might have been sent to dozens, perhaps hundreds, of companies will get you nowhere. However, something along the lines of "I recently read that you are planning to expand your operations and so I am writing to see if you have any openings for . . .", or "I was playing golf with your MD, who suggested I got in touch" shows an effort on your part to connect to that particular reader.

2. **Make the pitch:** Describe what can you offer the company. Try to make sure that every point you make is likely to be relevant to their needs.

3. **Where to from here:** manage the process by saying what you want to happen next. Something like "I'll call you in a week's time to see if there might be value in meeting up" or a less pushy "I look forward to hearing from you." With either of these options, follow up with a telephone call if you've heard nothing after ten days or so.

The shortlisting process

A reader's letter to *The Independent* (11 March 2000) claimed that a Hull-based personnel department takes the following approach to short-listing job candidates:

> First, we take out all the ones who are unemployed and put them in the bin. Then we take out all the women and put them in the bin. Then we take out all the ex-servicemen and put them in the bin. Then we take out all the ones over 40 and put them in the bin. Then we look at what's left.

Most professional recruiters would totally disown that practice. What is more normal is for a set of criteria to be drawn up for a vacancy against which each CV or application form is assessed. On this basis, the applicants are often sifted into "Must Sees", "Maybes", and "Definitely Nots", with the "Maybes" either being held in reserve or added to the "Must Sees" pile if it's a bit on the low side.

Preparing for an interview

If you are invited to an interview, you'll normally have a week or two to wait before the interview itself. This period is one of the most crucial parts of the whole process. Used well, you can give yourself a real chance to distinguish yourself on the day of the interview.

As job-hunting has become ever more competitive, candidates should always be on the lookout for opportunities to separate themselves from the pack. The quality of your preparation for an interview is such an opportunity.

Find out as much as you possibly can about the company. Some suggestions on how to do this:

- Work your networks and you can often amaze yourself with who you know who either works for the company, or is a customer a supplier.

- Get hold of an annual report. This can often be done on-line either via the company's website or using a service like the *Financial Times*' Annual Reports service, operated by WIL-Link (go to www.worldinvestorlink.com where you can select as many reports as you want, type in your address and the reports will be sent to you free of charge). Alternatively, phone the companies direct and ask them to send you a copy.

- Talking of company websites, most companies of any kind of size will have one. The best sites have an online copy of annual reports, information on company structures, copies of vision or mission statements, news releases, and links to related sites. If you don't know the website address, it's always worth trying www.(insert name of company here).co.uk or .com. Failing that, a decent search engine will get you there pretty quickly. If there isn't a company website, that also tells you a lot.

- Scan the newspapers if you can, particularly the broadsheets, and particularly on the day of the interview. If something is in the papers, chances are that the topic may well be high in the minds of people who work there – and at the very least you show you have a good grasp of current business news.

The other important element of your preparation to focus on is your interview strategy, for example:

- What are the key points you want to get over at the interview? Once you have identified these, treat them as a mental checklist to take along with you to the meeting.

- What are the interviewer(s) likely to want to know about you – start to map out how you might respond to these questions if they were to come up. In particular, anticipate the inevitable question "Why have you applied for to us?" But don't memorize your responses word for word – coming back with all-too-clever and obviously rehearsed responses will win you few friends.

- Prepare a few questions to ask at the end of the interview.

Q: Is there a company out there that will recognize my talents

A: Only if you take personal responsibility for marketing your skills, experience, and personal qualities. Nobody else is likely to do it for you.

SMART
ANSWERS
TO TOUGH
QUESTIONS

On the day of the interview

- Arrive early, sit in reception and just observe what goes on. Watch out for simple things like whether you seem to be expected, whether you get a friendly greeting and the offer of a cup of coffee, how the receptionist generally greets visitors, or what sort of conversations they have with colleagues passing by the desk.

- Check out any corporate literature that might be available in the reception area. You can often glean very helpful information this way. For example, a front page of the company newsletter devoted to a team of the month award tells you something about the organization's values and aspirations. On the other hand, if the front page is devoted to a dry-as-tinder address by the CEO exhorting the troops to tighten their belts, it's another pretty clear, if less positive, indication of what you might be letting yourself in for.

- Don't be alarmed if you feel a little anxious. Pre-interview nerves can serve a positive purpose by helping us to perform. If, however, you tend to suffer from extreme levels of nervousness, try using positive visualization techniques to help you imagine the event going well. Alternatively, get the occasion into perspective by asking yourself what is the worst that can happen. Do you remember Boris Becker being interviewed at Wimbledon after going out of the competition at a very early stage, and saying something like "I lost a tennis match. It wasn't a war. Nobody got killed"?

SMART VOICES

In a *Guardian* interview (27 January 2001), Anne Hollier of the Chartered Institute of Personnel and Development advises intending interviewees to make themselves familiar with the latest business jargon: "core competences" instead of skills, "working outside one's comfort zone" instead of being flexible. Being unaware of phrases in everyday use in a particular industry shows a lack of research.

What to wear to an interview

You never get a second chance to make a first impression. OK, it's a cliché but sometimes clichés are clichés because they're true. If you turn up for an interview wearing clothes that fitted you perfectly in the pre-paunch 1980s, with evidence of that morning's breakfast mingling with your ZZ Top beard, whiffing gently of last night's garlic bread and sporting a hairstyle borrowed from Tom Hanks in the latter stages of *Castaway*, you can pretty much kiss that job goodbye.

As a general guideline, it's better to overdress than under. Should you arrive for an interview turned out in a suit to be greeted by your new potential boss in a casual sweater, it's plausible to say that you're in your smart gear because you're going to a formal meeting after the interview.

Telling a smart suit that you're wearing jeans because you're planning to scrub the kitchen floor later than day lacks credibility.

Aim to enter the room confidently. Try to convey energy and positive enthusiasm. Make eye contact with the interviewer(s). Smile. When you sit down, go for relaxed but attentive – you might try crossing your feet at the ankles and keeping your hands in your lap. Try to get a dialogue going. Allow yourself thinking time if you need it.

Smart things to say about your career

Handling the interview

Don't undersell yourself

At your current employer, it may well be that you have a file full of appreciative letters from satisfied customers, that you've had a string of highly complimentary appraisals from a succession of managers, or that you're cheered to the rafters by your colleagues every time you enter the canteen because you're so damned good. At the interview, it's just you. Alone. Solo. There's no chorus of supporters to yell out that you're underselling yourself. To put it succinctly, interviews are not the time for disarming modesty on your part. The fact that you might in reality be the best candidate by a long shot counts for nothing. What you don't tell the interviewer, they will never know.

Don't oversell yourself

Equally well, don't dress up or exaggerate your experience. Implying that you led a project team when your main contribution was to fetch in the team's burgers at lunchtime is a recipe for disaster. A good, probing interviewer will find you out rapidly, leaving you feeling sheepish at best and deeply embarrassed at worst. There is also an outside chance that you might manage to talk yourself into being offered a job that you don't have the skills or experience to make a success.

Be honest

Avoid telling downright lies. On the other hand, don't give an exhaustive guide to all the skeletons in your closet. This is not the moment to tell everybody your party piece anecdote about how you came by your drink-driving ban.

Don't fake anything: it's better to lose a job offer by being yourself than it is to receive offer pretending to be something you're not. Not all jobs are going to be right for you. Chances are if you've presented a distorted

How to manage professional recruiters

Professional recruiters fall in to three categories: headhunters, search and selection businesses, and high street agencies. There is arguably a fourth group emerging who specialize in the interim marketplace, but these are often a subset of search and selection businesses.

High street agencies normally deal in lowish-level posts and temporary positions. They are worthwhile points of contact for anybody seeking manual, administrative, or secretarial roles.

Headhunters are commissioned by companies to find senior executives with a particular set of attributes. They assemble a shortlist of people with the best fit and receive a fee (typically an agreed a percentage of the job's salary and benefit's package). The shortlist is often a combination of candidates who respond to advertisements placed by the headhunters, people who have directly approached the headhunters, and those sought out by the headhunting company on the basis of recommendation by other parties.

Search and selection businesses usually focus on middle to senior level vacancies. Their client base tends to be a combination of people responding to advertisements and those who approach them directly.

Whereas high street agencies are happy for people to walk in off the street, the preferred *modus operandi* for headhunters and search and selection businesses is to receive the CV first, followed by a meeting. That said, it can be productive to walk in off the street to personally deliver a CV.

People using any professional recruiter need to be aware that these companies consider themselves client-driven, not candidate-driven, i.e. they are working primarily for companies and not for you. As a result, it can feel like you are not getting much of a service from them. Even though they stand to make a sizeable commission out of placing you, you may find they are sometimes too busy to talk to you.

The key to success here is for you to take responsibility for managing the relationship. Don't risk dropping off their radar by assuming they are actively putting you forward for jobs. Give them a call every ten days or so to see how what's around. Even if you are registered with them, when you see an advertisement they have placed that could suit you, contact them to explicitly state your interest in being considered.

picture of who you are and what you want, you're going to end up miserable in the job sooner or later.

Handling questions about salary

Perhaps you earned a fortune in your last job and don't want to price yourself out of the market. Before you start trying to talk your salary down, make sure you have up-to-date information about industry salary norms (job advertisements in the papers or on the internet are often good sources). If you know anybody who works for your prospective

Colleen Aylward, a highly experienced web recruiter, has created all kinds of tactics to attract and to evaluate talent. And she's heard just about every interview question ever asked. Here are 10 questions that she believes will always get you the information that you need.

1. Take me through a time when you took a product or a project from start to launch.
2. Describe the way that you work under tight deadlines.
3. Describe how you work under tough managers.
4. What is your definition of working too hard?
5. Persuade me to move to your city.
6. How do you manage stress?
7. What kinds of opportunities have you created for yourself in your current position?
8. In a team environment, are you a motivator, a player, a leader, or an enthusiast?
9. In the past three years, what part of your professional skill set have you improved the most?
10. If you were a new employee, what would you do to gain respect from peers in 30, 60, or 90 days?

Fast Company, June 2000

employers, check out with them typical levels of salary offered. Consider the following:

- Your previous company was noted for paying above market rate salaries.

- The salary offered is only one consideration in taking a position – opportunities for personal and career development, to cut down commuting time, work flexible hours might be just as important.

Be warned, though, about dropping your salary. It's hard to argue that you are worth £50k a year when three months before you accepted a £40k job because you needed the money

Use of humour

There are few better ways of bonding with somebody than through a joke shared. But be warned. If you're asked a difficult question, giving the response "Can I phone a friend/ask the audience?" might get a smile of recognition from the interviewer if they're a regular viewer of "Who Wants to be a Millionaire" but there are still plenty of people around whose cultural reference points begin and end with Radio 3 and whose response to your piece of wit will fall somewhere between an old-fashioned quizzical look and a surreptitious press of the security button under the interview table.

Q: How do you handle a question asking about your weaknesses?

A: When asked to describe a weakness, it's not clever to come back with "I can't think of one." You'll be marked down as lacking self-knowledge at best, and as an arrogant SOB at worst. Once, the optimal response was to offer a weakness that is strength in disguise. For example: "I'm not too good at time management — I'll always take time out to help a colleague who's struggling, and as a result I sometimes fall a bit behind with my own workload, although I'll always stay late that day if I need to catch up." Responses like this – sometimes called "the noble weakness" - can still work well. However, these days, it's reckoned that refreshing honesty like "My spelling's abysmal" might just be the best policy . . . just as long as you don't present a weakness that will have your interviewer seriously doubting your suitability to join their company.

SMART ANSWERS TO TOUGH QUESTIONS

Be positive

Don't tell a potential employer that you want to move on because you can't stand the people you're working with. Also, try to give some measurable indications of your positive impact, e.g. by instituting a "lights out before lunch" campaign I reduced the company's electricity bill by 20%

Asking questions

Some questions you might like to ask: What's the most exciting thing about working here? And what's the worst? What are the biggest challenges facing this part of the business over the next year or so? What do your customers think of you?

A word of warning for the interviewer

When you have an interview with someone and have an hour with them, you don't conceptualize that interview as taking a sample of the person's behavior, let alone a biased sample, which is what it is. What you think is that you are seeing a hologram, a small and fuzzy image but still the whole person.

Richard Nisbett, a psychologist at the University of Michigan, quoted in an article "The New-Boy Network" from *The New Yorker*, 29 May 2000

After the interview

Oh dear, your interview was three weeks ago and you haven't heard anything since. Try to avoid this situation arising by clarifying while you're at the interview what the next step in the process and the likely timescale for hearing how you've got on.

> **Interview blunders**
>
> Here are five ways to reduce your chances of getting the job you always wanted
> - Arrive unprepared
> - Wear the wrong clothes
> - Talk too much
> - Undervalue or overvalue yourself
> - Act as though you're desperate for the job

When you get back home, consider dropping a line to the interviewer reconfirming your interest in the job. Enclose any information that you may have promised

Spend a bit of time reviewing your performance: Did you talk too much? Did you find any questions particularly difficult to answer? What went well/badly? Any lessons to learn for the next interview you attend?

> Success in the job search process is typically not about being head and shoulders above all other candidates – it's about being a few per cent better than the competition every step of the way. Having a CV that conveys your experience and achievements more effectively, researching a company that bit more thoroughly, being that bit better prepared for the interview, making a better first impression than others, etc.

Smart things to say about your career

Assessing the job offer

According to a 2001 survey by Hay Management Consultants, 45% of a sample of 247 senior managers said that they should have spent more time and effort investigating new jobs before accepting them. Another survey – this time by online recruitment service totaljobs.com – reports that 10% of new starters walk out of work before finishing their first day, 14% leave in less than a week, and 17% fail to complete a month.

Leaving one job for another is a significant life decision. An informed decision is always likely to yield a better outcome than a leap into the dark. Before you think of resigning, are you confident that you know enough about the new role and the new company – its culture, the state of the balance sheet, and so on? If the offer has come from a dot.com, for example, how does the fact that over 200 of them closed in the first four months of 2001 affect your judgement?

If you're without a job at present, ask yourself your reasons for thinking about accepting an offer. Taking a job simply to end a period of ambiguity and uncertainty in your career may just be storing up trouble for later. To be looking for another job six months after starting with a new company poses a challenge for your CV and your interview technique and raises questions about either your judgement or your commitment. Far better to get it right first time.

So remember that you're not obliged to accept the first job offer that comes your way. The offer may be flattering but you are free to turn it down if it's a poor fit for the criteria you've established for your ideal job – salary level, degree of challenge in the role, location, future prospects, and so on. On the other hand, when an offer meets most, but not all, of your criteria, you may choose to accept it or see if you can improve the offer through discussion

Interim management

Over the past few years, an increasing number of managers have been going down the interim management route as an alternative to looking for a permanent job. In a nutshell, interim management involves the engagement of a senior executive by a company to undertake a significant assignment for a limited period of time, on average around six months.

As well as being used in an emergency, interim managers are increasingly being used out of choice. When it comes to change management, they are often favoured over consultants and permanent staff. It is said that they differ from consultants because typically the interim manager is there to implement rather than recommend. A recent Mori survey commissioned by Board Level Interim Executive found that only 9% of analysts and 26% of investors thought consultants were more effective and suitable for change projects than interim's.

Slimmed-down organizations and flat hierarchies are also creating work for interims. According to Andrew Pullman, head of HR for global markets at Dresdner Kleinwort Benson: "Nowadays there are no spare managers hanging around with nothing to do. The good thing about an interim manager is that you can parachute them in if there is a project that needs doing. You know that you'll get a good-quality result and that there will be minimal fuss."

Negotiating a better deal

- Always aim to negotiate with the decision-maker rather than through intermediaries.

- It's always preferable to negotiate on the basis of having received a written offer. Not only will this help to prevent misunderstandings, but it also helps to depersonalize the situation if you are negotiating over a piece of paper. Remember that you are often dealing with somebody that could soon be your new boss. It pays not to antagonize them.

- Keep the negotiation in a positive climate by reaffirming your real interest in joining the company, by emphasizing how pleased you were to receive the offer, and by looking forward to working with the new company – it's just a matter of clearing up a few contractual points to everybody's satisfaction.

- If you're going to negotiate, you'll need to make a case setting out your reasons why you would like the company to consider revising their offer. Try to give the company a few options to respond to rather than box yourself into a corner.

- Don't let the process drag on. Aim to negotiate crisply and settle quickly.

- If you decide to reject the job offer, keep it courteous and professional. Remember that the people you are dealing with are probably good networkers also; the last thing you want is to be bad-mouthed within your industry for buggering people about. For that reason, drop the company a line saying that you were pleased to have been offered the job, but that you regret that you can't accept the offer. Give your reasons why, thank them for taking the time to meet with you, and wish them well with filling the post.

Managing references

Most potential employers still seek written references before confirming a job offer. It has become usual for references to be fairly bland in tone.

Presidents and prime ministers place great emphasis on the impact they can make in their first 100 days. It's a period of heightened interest for the media and the voters, and a good launch can create a positive impetus for the remainder of their term of office. The same principles apply when you start the new job. Your boss, your colleagues, your team, and possibly the whole organization will be watching you in the early days. First impressions count. Any honeymoon period can be very short-lived.

- Be visible – get out and meet as many people as possible.

- Find out who's who, get to grips with company polices and procedures absorb as much as you can as quickly as you can.

- Don't refer to your former organization as 'we'; in fact, only refer to your past experience if it's relevant.

- Be guarded about your views – there will be plenty of organizational hot potatoes and people will be trying to recruit you to their various causes or grievances.

- Make something happen as soon as you can. If your 100 days have passed and the impression people get is that little if anything has changed, then you've missed a trick.

Nonetheless, it is worth putting a bit of care into identifying people who are well placed to comment positively on you and the contribution you have made. Ideally, have a range of possible referees on the stocks so that you can put the most appropriate list up to the company that wants to take you on.

Exiting with style

When it comes to handing in your notice at your current employers, bear in mind that the way we leave a company speaks volumes about the way we value work, our colleagues, and our reputation. Leave with good grace: buy the doughnuts, and the round of drinks; go round the office to personally say goodbye to both the people you liked and the people who would like to speak well of you; don't lace any farewell speeches with vitriol – you are not going to endear yourself to your imminently former colleagues by telling how glad you are to be moving on and what mugs they are for staying there.

Interlude 3

The Ten Stages of a Career

Edgar Schein

Edgar Schein, professor of management at the Sloan School of Management, Massachusetts Institute of Technology, has suggested that a career consists of several discrete stages, which provide us with a kind of internal timetable.

The stages can be long or short, the length of time associated with each stage varying widely according to the nature of the occupation and the individual in it. The stages can repeat themselves if the person moves from one career to another, and are not related necessarily to age.

SMART
PEOPLE
TO HAVE
ON YOUR
SIDE

The ten stages identified by Schein are:

1. Growth, fantasy, and exploration

2. Education and training

3. Entry into the world of work

4. Basic training, socialization

5. Gaining of membership

6. Gaining of tenure, permanent membership

7. Mid-career crisis, reassessment

8. Maintaining momentum, regaining it, or levelling off

9. Disengagement

10. Retirement

Stage 1: Growth, fantasy, and exploration – In this period, usually associated with childhood and early adolescence, an occupation is a mere thought and a career has little meaning except in terms of occupational stereotypes and a general goal of "success".

Stage 2: Education and training – Depending on the occupation, this can lasting anything from a few months to 20 or more years. In some occupations (such as medicine), the external career stages require early decision making to ensure that all of the prerequisites for later entry are achieved during the period of education.

Stage 3: Entry into the world of work – A time of major adjustment as people learn about the realities of work and their own reactions. They begin to test their talents, motives, and values in the crucible of real work.

Stage 4: Basic training and socialization – The length and the intensity of this period differ by occupation, organization, and the complexity of the work. In this stage, the organization begins to make demands to which the individual must respond. There are real choices to be faced about whether or not to remain in the occupation.

Stage 5: Gaining of membership – At some point, individuals recognize that they have passed beyond the trainee stage and have been accepted as a full contributor. At this stage a meaningful self-image as a member of the occupation or organisation begins to emerge. By now, people have a better sense of one's talents, strengths, and weaknesses.

Stage 6: Gaining of tenure and permanent membership – Within the first 5–10 years of a career, most organizations and occupations make a tenure decision that tells the individual whether or not he or she can count on a long-term future in the organization. In most organizations the process is not that formalized but operates nevertheless through norms pertaining to seniority or layoffs.

Stage 7: Mid-career crisis and reassessment – There is mounting evidence, says Schein, "that most people go through some kind of reassessment of themselves when they are well into their careers, asking themselves questions about their initial choices ('Have I entered the right career?'), about their levels of attainment ('Have I accomplished all I hoped to accomplish?' or 'What have I accomplished and was it worth the sacrifices?'), and about their futures ('Should I continue or make a change?' or 'What do I want to do with the rest of my life, and how does my work fit into it?'). Such reassessment can be traumatic, but many people find it to be normal and relatively painless, often leading to a rediscovery or re-affirmation of goals."

Stage 8: Maintaining momentum, regaining it, or levelling off – After stage 7, this is the point at which people make decisions about how the remainder of their careers will be played out. As Schein puts it: "For some this is a determination to climb the ladder as far as possible; for some it is a redefining of the areas of work they wish to pursue; and for many it involves a complex assessment of how to balance the demands of work, family, and personal concerns."

Stage 9: Disengagement – At this stage, people typically slow down, become less involved, and begin to think about retirement. However, some people deal with potential retirement by aggressively denying its reality.

Stage 10: Retirement – Whether or not the individual has prepared for it, inevitably the organization or occupation no longer makes a meaningful role available and the individual must adjust. Some retire early because they want to or because that's the norm for the occupation (e.g. the military or professional sports); for others, retirement is traumatic, resulting in loss of physical or psychological health, sometimes to the point of premature death.

Derived from Edgar Schein, *Career Anchors: Discovering your Real Values* (Jossey-Bass Pfeiffer, 1990)

5

Roads Less Travelled By

Two roads diverged in a wood, and I –
I took the one less travelled by,
And that has made all the difference
>From "The Road Not Taken" by Robert Frost

According to research, almost 16% of the UK workforce is self-employed, compared with 14% in the USA.
>Guardian, 2 May 2001

The trouble with the rat race is that even if you win, you're still a rat.
>Actress Lily Tomlin

This chapter looks at the career options available to those who choose to jump the corporate ship, or indeed an increasing number of people who are making a point of never getting on board in the first place.

Specifically, we will be covering:

• *What's involved in setting yourself up in business*

• *Putting together a portfolio career*

We'll also take a quick peek at issues involved in taking out a franchise

It's obviously going to be a different kind of world in the next century. . . . It will be a world of fleas and elephants, of large conglomerates and small individual entities, of large political and economic blocs and small countries. The smart thing is to be the flea on the back of the elephant. Think of Ireland and the EU, or consultants and the BBC.

A flea can be global as easily as one of the elephants but can more easily be swept away. Elephants are a guarantee of continuity but fleas provide the innovation. There will also be ad hoc organizations, temporary alliances of fleas and elephants to deliver a particular project.

Charles Handy writing in the October 1999 edition of CBI News

Setting yourself up in business

Look, this is not intended to be a comprehensive step-by-step guide to the mechanics of setting up and running your own business (for that, I would recommend something like the Lloyd's TSB Small Business Guide *by Sara Williams, published by Penguin and updated annually). Rather, my intention is to highlight some of the key issues and choice-points that are involved.*

According to a report by NatWest Bank, we are currently seeing around 400,000 new businesses being launched each year in the UK.

A new business can be anything from maintaining gardens for people living in your neighbourhood, through to setting up your own dotcom with a potential world-wide market. You may be your business's only employee or you could have a number of people working for you.

Whatever the business and whatever its size, there are a few unavoidable truths about what will determine the success or failure of your enterprise.

In *The Death of Distance*, Frances Cairncross describes how, by using technology creatively, small companies can now offer services that, in the past, only giants could provide. What's more, the cost of starting new businesses is declining, and so more small companies will spring up. Many companies will become networks of independent specialists; more employees will therefore work in smaller units or alone.

Individuals with valuable ideas can attract global venture capital. Perhaps one of the most telling features of the new economy is that increasing numbers of people can describe themselves without irony as one-person global companies.

You've doubtless heard some of the horror stories about the number of new businesses that fold within a few years, sometimes just a few months. The bad news is that the stories are pretty much true. On average, 20% of new businesses crumple within 12 months, with over 50% disappearing within three years.

KILLER QUESTIONS

Do you really want to run
your own business?
Are you serious or just
curious about taking
the plunge?

In the *Lloyd's TSB Small Business Guide*, Sara Williams give a number of reasons why new businesses can go to the wall:

- Overestimating sales and underestimating how long it takes to achieve them

- Underestimating costs

- Failing to control costs ruthlessly

- Losing control over cash, i.e. carrying too much stock, allowing customers too long to pay, paying suppliers too promptly

- Failing to identify your market because of inadequate market research

- Failing to adapt your product to meet customer needs and wants

- Lacking sufficient skills in one of the following areas – selling and marketing, financial, production, technical

- Failing to build a team that is compatible and complementary, if your business is on a larger scale

- Taking unnecessary risks

- Underpricing

So far, so depressing. What do you have to do to give your business a fighting chance of surviving?

The fundamental equation for business success is a simple one. You need two elements in place:

1. You need a marketplace that makes a positive judgement about quality and value of your offering; and

2. You need to achieve a healthy cashflow.

However, behind these elements are a whole set of factors that you'll need to think about . . .

SMART QUOTES

> The most impressive entrepreneurs do not simply move quickly to exploit a market that everyone thinks they can see. That was one of the problems with the first wave – or perhaps herd – of e-commerce companies. They all galloped in the same direction. Entrepreneurs go against the flow. . . . Entrepreneurship is not just about speed; its about doing something different.
>
> The Industry Standard Europe, 7 December 2000

Would you give you a job?

One of the unusual facets of deciding to set up your own business is that you decide exactly what it is that you want to do. You are not bound by predefined organizational structures and job descriptions as you typically would be within a salaried corporate role. If you decide that you want to set up a business selling doughnuts to supermodels, that's what you can have a go at doing. Alright, so the laws of the marketplace and a dash of common sense would tell you that the idea is doomed, but that's not the point just now. The point is that you make that choice.

The other novel aspect of going self-employed is that you are the recruitment manager and the candidate rolled up into one. Unless you need to borrow money to finance your idea, you are the person that makes the final decision about your suitability to start and run your own business. The fact is that not everybody is cut out to be self-employed, not everybody has an entrepreneurial streak. So do you know yourself well enough to make the right decision?

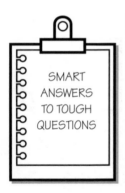

Q: Self-employment – is it for me?

A: Not everybody is cut out for self-employment. Somebody whose primary talent is for managing and inspiring others may find that working in an organization is more likely to provide the platform for exercising those skills. Similarly, somebody who places a high value on security could find the self-employed life just a little too fraught with risk for their liking. If you are not sure about self-employment, revisit Chapter 2 "Taking Stock". Reflecting on your output from the exercises should give you some pointers. Alternatively, take soundings from people that know you and whose judgement you trust.

Finally, to help you make up your mind, here are 12 smart questions gleaned from the Lloyd's TSB Small Business Guide:

1. Do you find it easy to approach people you do not know?

2. Do you have a wide circle of friends and acquaintants?

3. Do you enjoy working, with the general public?

4. Do you recover quickly from setbacks and rejections?

5. Are you a self-starter who works well on your own initiative?

6. Are you a good leader, organizer, and manager?

7. Are there any tasks which you hate doing but may find necessary if you are working for yourself

8. Do you find it easy to work long hours for protracted periods (days, weeks, even months)?

9. Are your health and energy levels good?

10. Can you rely on the support of your family

11. Are you good at getting the best out of people but tough with others when required?

12. Are you prepared to make sacrifices to succeed?

What's the big idea?

Remember the character played by Kevin Costner in the movie *Field of Dreams* who felt impelled to build a baseball stadium in the middle of nowhere on the basis of advice from a mystical friend that "If you build it, they will come"? I know people who have started a business on that basis – creating a market that never existed before in the belief that people will find the proposition irresistible.

On the other hand, it is quite a tall order to invent an entirely new business proposition. Most new businesses involve people deciding to sell familiar products and services – child-care, office cleaning, organic vegetables, CDs, house decorating, and so on.

In case you're struggling to come up with something suitable, here are 60 business ideas that have the additional merit of costing very little to set up:

Accountancy services	Dog training	Photographer
Aerobic instructor	Drawing cartoons	Private investigator
Air conditioning maintenance	Driver	Proof-reading

Aquarium maintenance	First aid instructor	Rare book locator
Astrology	Freelance writing	Relocation service
Auctioneer	Furniture repair	Reunion planning
Basket weaving	Graphic design	Services for the elderly
Bicycle repair and sales	Handyman	Sandwich service for offices
Business consultant	House-sitting	Second-hand dealer
Career counselling	Image consultant	Self publishing
Carpet cleaning	Interior design	Shopping service
Child care	IT skills training	Teaching English to foreign students
Children's performer	Mail order service	Trainer
Conducted walking tours	Mail handling service	Typing services
Cooking for parties	Manicurist	Upholstery cleaning
CV writing service	Message answering service	Videotaping service
Dance instructor	Musician/music teacher	Website designer
Dating agency	Party organizer	Wedding planner
Delivery service	Personal coach	Window cleaner
DJ	Pet care service	Yoga instructor

Of course, there are thousands of other potential business ideas you could consider, as a few minutes spent flicking through Yellow Pages would confirm.

Smart things to say

Don't assume that if you understand the technical work of a business, you understand a business that does technical work. They are two entirely different things. For the barber that starts their own business, suddenly the job he knows how to do well (i.e. cutting hair) becomes just one part of a bigger business, most of which he may well know next to nothing about.

The point is that just about any skill has a potential market. Once you've identified some ideas for your own business, you need to consider the following distinctions:

- Some ideas have long-term potential, others may only be short-lived.

- Some could earn you hundreds of pounds a day, others just a few quid.

- Some involved being based at home, others not.

- Some involve a lot of contact with other people, others are more solitary.

- Some will require constant updating of your knowledge, others are more static.

The clearer you are about your business idea, and the better thought through it is, the more likely you are to bring it successfully into being. As a general guideline, using an established skill, product, or knowledge, gives you the greatest chance of success. Again, it makes good sense to talk through your ideas with other people.

SMART
ANSWERS
TO TOUGH
QUESTIONS

Q: Should I produce a business plan?

A: If you want to borrow money to help finance your business, then you'll find it very difficult to get a loan without one. If you don't need to borrow and you have absolute clarity about your way forward, or if you're happy to try an idea on a 'suck it and see' basis, then spend your time on something else.

Do some market research

Does anybody want your service or product?

Say your ambition is to open a coffee bar. If there are already five coffee bars in the road you're looking at, does the world need a sixth? Conversely, if there are no coffee bars, how do you know that it's a great business opportunity rather than that there is simply no demand?

The answer is to carry out some market research. Dig around a bit. A genuine gap in the market is rare.

SMART
ANSWERS
TO TOUGH
QUESTIONS

Q: Do you want to run a business or be a business?

A: It's important to appreciate the distinction between self-employment and running a business.

Many people who become self-employed are simply looking to find work for themselves; they are happy as long as they are getting sufficient work to keep themselves as busy as they want, and to earn the income they need. Come the day that they decide to stop working, their business also ceases.

That approach is fine and dandy and suits many people. It does, however, involve a very different mindset to the person who is looking to build a business, which may in time develop the capability to run independently of the person who set it up.

It's the difference between being the 'MD of Me' and the MD of a business. As the 'MD of Me', you will probably be delivering all aspects of your business yourself. As the MD of a business, your prime focus will be building the business as effectively as possible. To achieve this, you may well want to draw on the services of other people.

When I started producing my magazine *Future Filter* back in 1996, I regarded it as my job to write, produce, and collate each edition. After all, it was my magazine, and I couldn't afford to pay for anybody else to work on it. Besides it very conveniently filled the cracks in my working week when there was no paid work to do for anybody else. If I was ill, then the magazine was delayed.

A couple of years ago, I changed my approach. I began to conceive of *Future Filter* as a brand to be developed rather than a way of occupying myself. Looking at myself as MD of *Future Filter*, I realized that my time was best spent editing and marketing the title rather than writing every word of it and personally printing off every copy.

So I brought on board some people to write material for the magazine. I farmed the magazine out to a local printer to produce on my behalf. The time I saved I devoted to building the readership.

Two years on, I have significantly increased the magazine's circulation, and there's every possibility that at some stage I could sell the magazine as a going concern to another business publisher.

Look, I'm no entrepreneur. And this is no huge success story. But it does illustrate the point that it pays to be very clear about what you want out of the work you do.

Weighing up the competition

If you are entering a crowded business arena, how will your competitors react? They may well have the resources to underwrite a price war against you. Are you resilient enough financially to deal with this?

Can the business support you from day one or would it make sense to keep the day job going, and hence some income coming in, while you build your business?

Do you need premises or could you keep running costs down by starting from a spare room?

Reality test your idea

Can you provide good-quality answers to these 10 questions? If you can't, there's a danger that your business idea won't work at all or won't work on a sustainable basis.

1. What is our offering?

2. Who are our customers?

3. What do they want?

4. What do I want out of my business?

5. What is the match between what I and the customers want?

6. How do they know about us?

7. How do they obtain our offering?

8. What is the current market?

9. What is the future market?

10. How will our offerings need to change?

Naming your business

Choosing the right name for your business is a key part of building your reputation.

As a sole trader or a partnership, you can more or less call yourself what you like. Your only problem would be if you were felt by another company to be trying to "pass yourself off" either as them or at least connected to them. Bill Gates would probably take umbrage if I were to set up a business called Microsoft Software.

Beyond that, you have a free hand. It's often worth thinking about what your product or service is, and then seeing if there is a way to encapsulate that idea in your business name. If you are setting up a niche consultancy, and you expect to be able to draw on your positive reputation in that field, you in effect are your own product and a name like *John Middleton and Associates* would be useful (although only, of course, if your name is John Middleton). Alternatively, you might want to embody your core service explicitly in your business name – *The Speedy Photocopying Centre*, *The Change People*, *Vegetables to Your Door*, that sort of idea. Before committing yourself to stationery, business cards, and the like, it's worth trying out your ideas for a name on potential buyers to see what impression it makes.

A few more tips:

- Avoid complicated names: you want to register a quick and positive impact.

- Avoid names with initials: they sound very formal and unapproachable. "A. and G. Roddick's" carries a very different feel to The Body Shop.

- Made-up words are growing more popular (not least because web search engines can find them easily), as are derivations of Latin words.

- Check your name in a few foreign dictionaries, particularly if you plan to trade overseas, to make sure your classy English name doesn't translate into something like "deeply unpleasant stomach bile".

If you are setting up a limited company, your hands are more tied. You will need to find a name that has not already been registered, that doesn't contain the word "limited" other than at the end, and that is not considered offensive.

Launching and marketing the business:

How do you plan to promote and market your business? More specifically, how are you going to locate your customers and then convince them that you're worth your salt?

Here are some possible answers:

- Networking

- Brochures and leaflets

- Press releases

- Write articles

- Give presentations for local groups

- Get yourself on the conference circuit

- Write a book

- Mail shots

- Placing advertisements

- Entries in relevant directories

Ooops, there go my pension and my life assurance

When you stop working for a company, they stop paying you a salary.

Alright, that may hardly qualify as a revelation, let alone a "smart thing", but less noticeable are a whole host of benefits that disappear along with your final pay cheque. The company pension goes, your death in service benefit goes, and you are no longer covered by group insurance schemes for public liability (the "health and safety" insurance that protects you and visitors to your company in the event of accidents).

When you set up on your own, there will be nobody to insist that you put in place a new pension plan, increase your life assurance cover, and so on. It becomes your call, and your call alone.

I have self-employed acquaintances who hold very different views in these areas. One person wouldn't dream of being without pension and life cover. Another has decided to invest in property rather than a pension. Yet another seems to be investing in cases of Margaux as a long-term moneyspinner.

You'll need to decide for yourself what your personal strategy will be.

Some areas may be less optional for you. Some public liability insurance will probably be required if the people need to visit your premises. You may also need it if you visit the premises of your clients/customers, say to service equipment.

Q: Should I take out professional indemnity insurance?

A: Definitely worth thinking seriously about, particularly if you are a consultant. These are increasingly litigious times, and it may happen that you will be sued for negligence at some time. The cost of cover starts at around £200–500 if you are covering just yourself. However, it's worth getting in contact with any professional institutes or associations that you belong to. They often have negotiated special rates for their members.

Forming a business - what legal structure should you adopt?

There are three main choices for the legal form of your business:

- Sole trader

- Partnership

- Limited company

Let's take each in turn,

Sole trader

In the UK, this is the quickest, cheapest, simplest, and by far the most common route to self-employment. It's estimated that around 70% of people who are self-employed are sole traders. Beyond notifying the tax and social security authorities that you are operating as a sole trader, there or no further specific legal requirements involved in setting up the business.

The advantages of being a sole trader:

- It involves minimum red tape.

- You need only produce simple, unaudited accounts.

- You pay lower National Insurance payments than you would as a limited company.

- It's very straightforward to convert to a limited company at a later date if you wish.

- Equally, it is very easy to wind up the business – there are no legal complications.

And the drawbacks:

- You and your business are not legally separate, and so you are personally liable for any business debts.

- You have limited flexibility on tax planning compared to being a limited company.

- You are not eligible to claim unemployment benefit if you cease trading.

- Some companies – particularly larger organizations – will only deal with limited companies.

Partnership

A partnership consists of two or more self-employed people who work together, sharing the profits (and the losses) of their business. It is normal, and highly recommended, to draw up a partnership agreement with the help of a solicitor to cover all potential problem areas.

The advantages:

- The level of statutory regulation is less than that for limited companies.

- Lower disclosure of information required than limited companies

- You pay lower National Insurance payments than you would as a limited company.

Drawbacks:

- All those that apply to the sole trader

- Each partner is liable for all partnership debts, even if the other partner caused them. The fancy name for this is "joint and several liability".

Limited company

A limited company is a separate legal entity, which is distinct from the directors, employees, and shareholders connected to the company. So, for example, a limited company can be sued or sue in its own right. A limited company needs to be formally registered, in the case of the UK with Companies House.

The advantages:

- Individuals normally have a limited liability for the debts of the company equal to the amount invested in the company by the individual to buy shares. "Normally" here means as long the company has not traded fraudulently or wrongfully, and individuals have not given a personal guarantee, say as security for a company overdraft.

- Limited company status gives a business more credibility.

- Shares can be used as an incentive for staff.

- The company itself may become a saleable asset over time.

- Historically, there have been tax advantages for high earners, who can make large pension contributions, keep money in the business, pay themselves dividends, etc.

Drawbacks:

- Forming a limited company can be a complicated and time-consuming process involving accountants and solicitors.

- Being a limited company involves increased regulation and "red tape", as does any decision to wind it up.

Setting a price

Because so many Smart Careerists go down the consultancy route, let's use the example of a business consultant to illustrate this point.

It is tempting when you start up as a consultant to set your prices based on the level of income you want to generate. It seems logical. You want to generate £50,000 a year and reckon you'll be able to achieve 100 days of chargeable work. Ergo, your daily rate is £500.

Very rational, very wrong.

What is missing from the equation is any sense of the price range that your customers would expect to pay. The question consultants need to ask themselves is, "What's the market rate for this type of work?" Think about it for a moment. Would you really rather work 100 days a year at £500 a day when you might be able to work 50 days at £1,000?

There's another question linked to this: how price sensitive are your customers? To put it a different way, to what extent would you lose customers by raising your prices, or gain them by reducing your charges? Consultancy is often a relatively insensitive market. People bring consultants into their companies to help them address thorny issues: getting a solution is typically more important than saving a few bob. Can you imagine a project manager being held to account by their MD for a poor result and saying of the consultants used: "Look I know that the consultants I selected have failed to deliver, but at least they were cheap!"

As a general guideline, consultants submitting proposals for work can afford to charge at the higher end of the price range. If the rate is genuinely problematic for a company, then the option is there for the consultants to drop their daily rate.

Curiously, perhaps, undercharging is more problematic than overcharging. The trouble with pricing low to get the business is that once you allow yourself to be secured at a knockdown price, your customers assume that is the rate that they can pay in the future.

The other irony of putting a low price on your services is that you fall through the floor of credibility. Particularly when it comes to hiring consultants, most companies have a sense of the going rate for the work on offer. If you charge significantly less than your competitors, the working assumption is not that you provide quality at a low price; rather it is that you lack the experience or gravitas to carry off the work required.

That's all very well for consultants, you might be thinking, but what happens in a more price-sensitive market. If you are convinced that the main factor in buying is price, then of course it makes sense to take a less cavalier approach. The key is knowing your marketplace and your customers.

B. Joseph Pine, II and James H, Gilmore, co-founders of Strategic Horizons LLP

Why does a cup of coffee cost more from a trendy café than it does from the street vendor or when made at home? Partly it's because of the inherent costs involved, but more significant is the nature of the experience and the value attached to it. So say Pine and Gilmore, who begin their book *The Experience Economy* (HBS Press, 1999) by taking the reader through the following life story of a coffee bean:

SMART
PEOPLE
TO HAVE
ON YOUR
SIDE

Companies that harvest coffee or trade it on the futures market receive – at the time of this writing – a little more than $1 per pound, which translates into one or two cents a cup. When a manufacturer grinds, packages, and sells those same beans in a grocery store, turning them into a good, the price to a consumer jumps to between 5 and 25 cents a cup (depending on brand and package size). Brew the ground beans in a run-of-the-mill diner, corner coffee shop, or bodega and that service now sells for 50 cents to a dollar per cup. So depending on what a business does with it, coffee can be any of three economic offerings – commodity, good, or service – with three distinct ranges of value customers attach to the offering. But wait: serve that same coffee in a five-star restaurant or espresso bar, where the ordering, creation, and consumption of the cup embodies a heightened ambience or sense of theatre, and consumers gladly pay anywhere from $2 to $5 for each cup. Businesses that ascend to this fourth level of value establish a distinctive experience that envelops the purchase of coffee, increasing its value (and therefore its price) by two orders of magnitude over the original commodity.

The coffee bean's journey from commodity, to good, to service, and finally to experience carries a telling moral: the most obvious and significant source of added value in this whole journey is the point at which the offering becomes an experience for the consumer.

And it's at this "fourth level of value" – the experience level – that companies have their biggest opportunity to distinguish themselves from their rivals.

Monitoring performance

Every six months, slot in half a day when you will take time out to assess your performance. Ask yourself the following questions (and a few of your own):

1. How is the business performing?

Q: How can I increase my profits?

A: You'll have to do one, and preferably all, of the following:

- Cut your costs.
- Increase your prices.
- Sell more.

It's also worth looking at a breakdown where your income is currently coming from and focusing on the higher-value areas. If you're a consultant and can earn £1,000 a day working in the financial sector, as opposed to £500 a day elsewhere, then it's pretty obvious – all else being equal — where you need to focus your marketing effort.

SMART
ANSWERS
TO TOUGH
QUESTIONS

2. Has everything gone to plan?

3. Have there been any surprises?

4. Any major disappointments to date?

5. Am I getting the level of income I need?

6. Am I getting the level of income I want?

7. Am I enjoying myself?

8. Do I need to do anything different over the coming months?

9. Shall I re-commit to this business for another six months?

Words from the wise

Over the past few years, I've been running *Starting Your Own Business* workshops at regular intervals. The following is a summary of some of the insights and advice offered by delegates:

1. Only you can decide whether you have the necessary qualities and abilities to make a success of self-employment. Identify your weaknesses and strengths.

2. Analyse what you expect and hope to achieve from self-employment. Make a point of having regular reviews to determine whether you're getting there.

3. Do not underestimate the problems and difficulties.

4. Don't feel obliged to be original. A well-worn idea can be successful.

5. Don't overlook the need to market because you are already too busy or overworked. If you do, you risk getting into a cycle of famine and feast

6. Remember that the market is crucial in determining your success or failure.

7. Expect everything to go wrong and plan for it by having alternatives already planned and ready for implementation when needed.

8. Improve your cashflow by avoiding or at least delaying every expenditure possible.

9. Work now and rest later.

10. Feel encouraged but don't be misled by client's promises of lots of business in the future.

11. Be known for doing what you say you will do, and doing it promptly.

12. Baden-Powell was right: be prepared. Flying by the seat of your pants is not the way to impress your customers.

13. Find out as much as you can about the company you are visiting and the person you want to impress.

14. Be totally businesslike in your dealings.

15. You need to gain credibility in your chosen field

16. Know your competition: anticipate their moves.

17. Get yourself a good accountant sooner rather than later

18. Charge what you're worth.

19. Try to find a business in a sector with real growth potential – it's no fun being a big fish in a shrinking pond.

20. Success today is no guarantee of success tomorrow.

SMART QUOTES

Honour your mistakes as hidden intentions.

Attributed to musician Brian Eno by Steve Erickson, *Uncut* magazine, June 1999

21. Make sure that you can tell people what you do clearly and succinctly, i.e. in no more than 15 seconds.

Franchising

When you buy a burger, take a suit or dress to a local drycleaner, get some papers photocopied, the chances are you'll be dealing with a franchised operation.

Franchising is when the owner of a business or product allows other people to market and sell the owner's products in return for payment. This normally amounts to a set-up fee as well as ongoing payments that are typically based on sales achieved. There may also be an agreed fee paid to the owner for providing training.

The advantages of franchising:

* The franchisee is buying into a proven business idea.
* On-going advice and support is provided.
* The franchise often has a recognized brand name
* No specific knowledge of the industry is needed as training is given.
* The franchisee can benefit from the greater bargaining power that franchisers have with suppliers.

The drawbacks:

* Franchisers, it has to be said, are pretty cute about the value or a franchise. You're unlikely to get a bargain.
* A franchise carries additional costs, especially at start-up
* A franchise can involve being tied in legally for a long period

Taking out a franchise is an option worth considering for anybody who wants to run their own business but who would feel reassured if they were trading in a recognized product or brand.

For more details about franchising, it is worth getting in touch with:

The British Franchise Association
Thames View
Newtown Road
Henley on Thames
Oxon RG9 IHG
Tel: 01491 578050
www.british-franchise.org.uk

Portfolio working

In the past, for most of us, our work portfolio has had only one item in it, at least for men. It was their job or, more grandiosely, their career. This was, when you think about it, a risky strategy. Few would these days put all their money into one asset, yet that is what a lot of us have been doing with our lives. That one asset, that one job, has had to work overtime for we have looked to it for so many things at once – for interest or satisfaction in the work itself, for interesting people and good company, for security and money, for the chance of development and reality.

Charles Handy, *The Age of Unreason* (1989)

SMART VOICES

When Charles Handy published *The Age of Unreason* in 1989, he was remarkably prescient in anticipating most of the key business movements of the 1990s – the growth of outsourcing, telecommuting, the intellectual capital movement, and the rise of knowledge workers, *inter alia*.

Just as crucially, Handy foresaw how these developments might impact on the individual. He predicted correctly that a full-time permanent job in an organization would become a minority occupation before the end of the 20th century. And it was his concept of the portfolio worker that arguably provided a way forward for that part of the whole downshifting movement of the nineties that was wrestling with redefining the nature of work as well as questions of life balance.

Corporate life spans are shrinking. Remember a little outfit called Netscape? Netscape was formed in 1994, went public in 1995, and was gone by 1999, subsumed into AOL's operation. This giant of the new economy reached only its fourth birthday. Question: Was Netscape a company – or was it really an extremely cool project? More important question: Does the distinction matter? Here's what does matter: That short-lived entity put several products on the market, prompted powerful companies (notably Microsoft) to shift strategies, and equipped a few thousand individuals with experience, wealth, and connections that they could bring to their next project.

The lesson: People, not companies, are "built to last." Most of us will outlive any organization for which we work.

Daniel Pink, writing in *Fast Company*, May 2001

According to Handy's definition, a work portfolio "is a way of describing how the different bits of work in our life fit together to form a balanced whole". Portfolio people, say Handy are "the sort of people who, when you ask them what they do, reply, 'It will take a while to tell you it all, which bit would you like?' Sooner or later, thanks to the re-shaping of the organization we shall all be portfolio people."

The categories of the portfolio

There are five main categories of work for the portfolio: wage *work* and *fee work*, which are both forms of paid work; homework *gift work*, and *study work*, which are all free work. Handy's definitions are as follows:

- Wage (or salary) work represents money paid for time given. Fee work is money paid for results delivered. Employees do wage work; professionals, craftspeople and freelancers do fee work. Fee work is increasing as jobs move outside the organization. Even some insiders now get fees (bonuses) as well as wages.

- Homework includes that whole catalogue of tasks that go on in the home, from cooking and cleaning, to children and cleaning, from carpentry to chipping. Done willingly or grudgingly, it is all work.

- Gift work is work done for free outside the home, for charities and local groups, for neighbours or for the community.

- Study work done seriously and not frivolously is, to me, a form of work not recreation. Training for a sport or a skill is study work, so is the learning of a new language or a new culture, so are the long days I spend reading other people's books in preparation for writing my own.

Where does the money come from?

That is always the central issue in planning a portfolio. Portfolio people think in terms of portfolio money not salary money. They learn that money comes in fits and starts from different sources. There may be a bit of a pension, some part-time work, some fees to charge or things to sell. They lead cash-flow lives not salary lives, planning always to have enough in-flows to cover out-flows.

Organizations were dreadful places in some ways, but they were places where companionship could be found. We will miss a lot of what organizations used to offer, the familiar faces we liked and the people we hated, the canteen and the gossip. Now we interact only with clients or our competitors. I think we have to have an alternative community of some sort, where we can refresh ourselves and relax. Because loneliness is to me one of the great sadnesses of portfolio life

Charles Handy, *The Search for Meaning*

Handy on portfolio thinking

- Portfolio people provide different services to different people, not one service.

- They know that most skills are saleable if you want to sell them. The fee can be as small, or as big, as you think fit; small for the first-time seller, big if you feel confident or if you do not really care whether you do it or you don't.

- Hobbies can be mini-businesses for portfolio people – cooking can be their skill, plants their merchandise.

- Portfolio people lead cashflow lives not salary lives, planning always to have enough in-flows to cover out-flows.

- Portfolio people think in terms of barter. They exchange houses for holidays, baby-sit for each other, lend garden tools in return for produce, give free lodging in return for secretarial help in the evenings.

- Portfolios should accumulate by choice, not chance. We can manage our time. We can say no. We can give less priority, or more, to homework or to paid work.

- Money is essential but more money is not always essential. Enough can be enough.

Good things about a portfolio career

- Choosing what to do and what not to do
- Meeting different people
- Variety
- The sense of freedom
- Plenty of stimulus – never being bored
- Being in control
- Being responsible
- Being institution-free
- Being appreciated and valued

Drawbacks

- Not having enough money
- Home being 90% about work – the office creeping into every corner

- Worrying about what the next steps are

- Financial and other fears

- Not having a central focus

- Managing priorities

- Explaining what a portfolio career is

- Overcommitment and worrying that there's not enough time to do it all

- Self-motivation and standing on own two feet after being in a corporate environment

- Loneliness

From *Portfolio People* by Max Comfort and *The Age of Unreason* by Charles Handy

---

Nine steps to financial freedom

1. Analyse your attitudes towards money and how they were shaped by childhood experiences.

2. Confront your deepest fears, whether of becoming a bag lady or simply failing behind on payments.

3. Do a two-year audit, working out exactly how much you spent and on what. If you spend more than you earn, what can you trim?

4. Be responsible: make a will, get a pension and life insurance.

5. Respect money. Don't waste it. Invest it. Cut up all credit cards.

6. Always trust your own instincts.

7. Don't be a cheapskate. Giving to charity will make you less anxious.

8. Accept that money has an ebb and flow.

9. Remember, true wealth has nothing to do with money.

Derived from Suze Orman, *The Nine Steps to Financial Freedom* (Crown, 1999)

6

Survival and Success in the New Work Economy

I believe that 90% of white-collar jobs in the US will either be destroyed or altered beyond recognition in the next 10 to 15 years. That's a catastrophic prediction, given that 90% of us are engaged in white-collar work of one sort or another.
  Tom Peters, "What Will We Do for Work?", *Time, 29 May 2000*

The Centre for Tomorrow's Company predicts that by 2025 the word "employee" will seem as dated as the term "domestic servant". Many companies have dispensed with "employees" and replaced them with "colleagues" and "associates".
                           Daily Telegraph, Friday 14th January 2000

It's difficult to make predictions – especially about the future.
Movie mogul Samuel Goldwyn

The manager's job is to thrive in a chaotic world they cannot control.
Theodore Zeldin, *An Intimate History of Humanity* (1994)

In the future – the not-too-distant future – only two groups of people will be in the world of work: entrepreneurs and those who think like entrepreneurs.
Terri Lonier, CEO of Working Solo Inc., quoted in *Fast Take Newsletter*, 7 March, 2000

The future of work

Trying to predict what the future world of work will hold for us all seems like a doomed pastime. It wasn't all that long ago that a technology-enriched future was going to bring prosperity for all, and with it, less hours at work, not to mention a life of leisure. Instead, people in the UK now work the longest hours in Europe and "a life of leisure" funded by being paid more for doing less seems like a pipedream.

One thing is certain: when it comes to the 21st century world of work, impermanence is in and "jobs for life" are out. As the writer Naomi Klein puts it in her book *No Logo* (Flamingo, 2000): "Offering employment – the steady kind, with benefits, holiday pay, a measure of security and maybe even union representation – has fallen out of economic fashion."

It's difficult to imagine a scenario in which "jobs for life" could make anything like a meaningful comeback. Companies lose money – and they purge staff. Companies announce record profits – and they purge staff. The correlation between company profit and job growth, according to Klein, has never been weaker.

Ten jobs that might disappear this decade

1. Stockbrokers, auto dealers, mail carriers, insurance and real estate agents: The Internet will eradicate millions of middle-men/women.

2. Teachers: Outsourcing the education system could be cheaper than installing metal detectors in schools.

3. Printers: Traditional printers may succumb to a combination of the development of digital paper technology, and high-quality, reasonably priced printers residing in businesses and homes.

4. Stenographers: To be replaced by increasingly sophisticated voice recognition software.

5. CEOs: The relentless pressure of the 24-hour business day will render single-voice, top-down decision-making increasingly cumbersome.

6. Orthodontists: 3-D computer simulation programs capable of cranking out disposable clear-plastic aligners to shift teeth into position are already in clinical trial.

7. Prison Guards: Microscopic implants will restrain convicts from taking part in criminal activity. Shades of *Clockwork Orange*?

8. Truckers: Motorways will have "smart" lanes capable of taking computer-driven vehicles driven bumper-to-bumper at high speed.

9. Housekeepers: Decision-making fridges today, self-motivated vacuum cleaners tomorrow?

10. Fathers: The male parent will succumb to developments in *in-vitro* fertilization and cloning (although who will fall asleep snoring in front of the television in the brave new world isn't yet clear).

Derived from an article in *Time* magazine, 29 May 2000

The war for talent

Paradoxically, at the same time as companies unload people in droves, a yearlong study conducted by a team from McKinsey & Co. involving 77 companies and almost 6,000 managers and executives has suggested that the most important corporate resource over the next 20 years will be talent: smart, sophisticated businesspeople who are technologically literate, globally astute, and operationally agile. And even as the demand for talent goes up, the supply of it will be going down.

The McKinsey team is blunt about what will result from these trends in its report entitled "The War for Talent". The search for the best and the brightest will become a constant, costly battle. Not only will companies have to devise more imaginative recruitment practices; they will also have to work harder to keep their best people. In the new economy, competition is global, capital is abundant, ideas are developed quickly and cheaply, and people are willing to change jobs often. In that kind of environment, says Ed Michaels, a McKinsey director who helped manage the study, "All that matters is talent. Talent wins."

So what are we to do?

At first sight, organizations are putting out mixed messages to the people that work for them. Do they want us or not? The increasing use of downsizing and outsourcing suggests they don't. The view of McKinsey and others that the coming decade will see companies trying to outbid and outperform each other in a war for talent suggests that organizations might need us after all.

Of course, these mixed messages are reconcilable. Organizations want some, but not all, of us, and they only want us if they perceive us as sources of added value; we are entering an era of conditional corporate love.

A survey in 1999 from the Institute of Directors and Development Dimensions International asked HR directors what percentage of their employees they would rehire if they could change all their employees overnight. Half said they would rehire between 0% and 40%.

Against this backdrop, the Smart Careerists who want to build their career within organizations need to develop for themselves (and regularly reinvent) a pool of skills and knowledge that will merit their place in a company's shrinking set of vital functions. Expressed at its highest level, Smart Careerists need to aim to become one of what writer Stuart Crainer calls the "Core Competents".

Crainer, in his excellent and highly readable book *A Freethinker's A–Z of the New World of Business*, has described how a relatively small number of executive high achievers increasingly hold corporate power.

According to Crainer, shortages of executive talent mean that the truly talented will have their choice of the plum roles. This, in turn, will mean that the old style administrator will become in less demand and will have to settle for positions below mahogany row. It will also spark a redefinition of what it means to be an executive.

Here's a brief extract from the book:

> For the select few, the world will be their oyster. Have talent; will travel. "Geography will be much less important in future. A new pattern of graduates and post-graduates is emerging," says Richard Wall

of headhunters Heidrick & Struggles. "But more to the point, there is much less of a country-focus to jobs. Executives are more willing to look cross borders. I think we are going to see a workforce which is much more transient, moving between companies and even continents."

Talented executives will be in demand and will be able to attract substantial salary and remuneration packages. In effect, corporate power will be concentrated in the hands of the few. "What is critical in the firm of the future is not so much the core competencies as the core competents," predicts Jonas Ridderstråle of the Stockholm School of Economics. "These walking monopolies will stay as long as the company can offer them something they want. When that is no longer the case, they will leave."

Ridderstråle points to a growing array of supporting evidence. Bill Gates has reflected that if 20 people were to leave Microsoft, the company would risk bankruptcy. In a study by the Corporate Leadership Council, a computer firm recognized 100 "core competents" out of 16,000 employees; a software company had 10 out of 11,000; and a transportation group deemed 20 of its 33,000 as really critical.

So few, yet so powerful. According to Randall E. Stross, professor of business at San Jose State University and a research fellow at Stanford University: "In the software industry, a single programmer's intellectual resources, through commercial alchemy, can create entire markets where none existed before. Compare the cumulative worldwide gross revenues of the studio that captures the next Steven Spielberg compared to the rival who has to settle for the second-round draft pick. Differences separating the rewards generated by the top tier versus the second tier are geometric, not arithmetic." At the top of the organization, that difference is likely to be exponential.

On the face of it, only the smartest of Smart Career-ists can become true Core Competents. So what are the rest of us to do?

Writer Rob Lieber, in an article in *Details* magazine back in June 1997, has an unequivocal response: "The time of considering yourself an 'employee' has passed. Now it's time to start thinking of yourself as a service provider, hiring out your skills and services to the highest, or most interesting, bidder."

We can also take on board six observations Thomas Stewart makes in his book *Intellectual Capital* about careers in the 21st century:

1. A career is a series of gigs, not a series of steps.

2. Project management is the furnace in which successful careers are made.

3. In the new organization, power flows from expertise, not from position.

4. Either insiders or outsiders can perform most roles in an organization.

5. Careers are made in markets not hierarchies.

6. The fundamental career choice is not between one company and another, but between specializing and generalizing.

If we want to make our careers outside of the corporate world, we can learn lessons from people like Charles Leadbeater who has written about a new and independent breed of cultural entrepreneurs that he calls 'The Independents' – see the side-panel below on Leadbeater for more detail.

Charles Leadbeater

Charles Leadbeater is an independent writer, a research associate for UK think-tank Demos, and a new economy consultant to leading companies. Previously, he was industrial editor and Tokyo bureau chief at the *Financial Times* before moving on the *Independent*, where he devised *Bridget Jones's Diary* with Helen Fielding. In 1998, he helped Peter Mandelson, then Secretary of State at the Department of Trade and Industry, to develop a White Paper entitled "Building the Knowledge Driven Economy".

In his best known book, *Living on Thin Air*, Leadbeater explores the societal implications of a knowledge-driven economy, coming as it does at a time of increasing economic and job insecurity. He argues that society will need to be organized around the creation of knowledge capital and social capital, rather than simply being dominated by the power of financial capital. "Knowledge," he writes, "is our most precious resource: we should organize society to maximize its creation and use. Our aim should be to harness the power of markets and community to the more fundamental goals of creating and spreading knowledge."

At a more practical level, he and Kate Oakley wrote a pamphlet called "The Independents: Britain's New Cultural Entrepreneurs" (Demos, 1999) in which they explore how a new breed of entrepreneurs are working from bedrooms and garages, workshops and run-down offices, hoping that they will come up with the next Hotmail or Netscape, the next Lara Croft, the next Wallace and Gromit, or Notting Hill.

This group – labelled *The Independents* by the authors – are typically in their twenties and thirties and have emerged from a convergence of three forces:

• Technology (the first generation that grew up with computers and that understand how to reap the benefits of modern computing power and communications).

- Values (typically anti-establishment, anti-traditionalist and highly individualistic – values that predispose them to pursue self-employment and entrepreneurship in a spirit of self-exploration and self-fulfilment).
- Economics (they have entered the workforce from the late 1980s onwards, during which time self-employment and entrepreneurship have become very attractive alternatives to careers in large, impersonal, frequently downsizing organizations).

This is an undeniably insightful and (I suspect in the long run) influential piece of writing, which contains this advice for the Smart Careerist on how to make it as an Independent:

1. Be prepared to have several goes: You're unlikely to make it first time around. Learn from failure, don't wallow in it.

2. Timing is critical: Technology is moving so fast that it's easy to be either too early or too late.

3. Don't have a plan: It will come unstuck because it's too inflexible.

4. Have an intuition and a feel for where the market is headed: Adapt and change with the consumers.

5. Be brave enough to be distinctive: If you are doing what everyone else is doing, you're in the wrong business.

6. Be passionate: If you don't believe in what you are doing, nobody else will. At the outset only passion will persuade other people to back you.

7. Keep your business lean: Buy top-of-the-range computers but put them on second-hand desks. Necessity is the mother of invention, not luxury.

8. Make work fun: If it stops being fun, people will not be creative.

9. Give your employees a stake in the business: You may not be able to pay them much to start with so give them shares.

10. Pick partners who are as committed as you: to start with, a business will only be sustained by a band of believers.

11. Don't be sentimental: Be ready to split with your partners – often your best friends – when the business faces a crisis or a turning point.

12. Create products that can become ubiquitous quickly: For example by being

given away in a global market, thereby attracting huge stock market valuations.

13. Don't aim to become the next Bill Gates: Aim to get bought out by him.

14. Take a holiday in Silicon Valley: You will be convinced anyone is capable of anything.

In the final analysis, whatever we choose to do with our careers, and wherever and however we choose to play them out over the coming years, one thing is absolutely clear: we can say goodbye to the job for life. And that is not necessarily bad news. As Tom Peters put it in *The Brand You 50*:

> It's over. Praise God its over. The world in which "we" – the best and the brightest, the college kids – depended on "them," the Big Companies to "guide" (micromanage! dictate! control!) "our" careers. Alas, my Dad was no more than an indentured servant to the Baltimore Gas & Electric Company for 41 years. Same door. West Lexington Street. Day after day. Month after month. Year after year. Decade after decade. It was no way to live, if living it were. But "It" is finished. Kaput.

7

A Final Word

Let's face it: the concept of a career, as understood by generations of workers before us, is dead and gone.

These days, the very idea that an individual can join a company from school or college and work their way up from office junior to president of the company just seems ridiculous. Besides, who would want to work in a company run by somebody who has never worked anywhere else? Who can even be confident that their company will be around long enough to underwrite that form of stately progression to the top? Thomas Stewart believes that, these days "you have a better chance of getting a gold watch from a street vendor than you do from a corporation".

No, my advice is unambiguous (and probably by now wholly predictable): Don't entrust your career to anybody.

Don't rely on the company's Management Development Manager or VP-Succession Planning to look after your interests – they have other fish to fry. Don't assume that being good at what you do is enough. Don't imagine that the skills and knowledge you have now will hold any value in the future. There is a line in an Elvis Costello song that expresses this well: today's news is tomorrow's fish and chip paper.

Above all, don't assume that combining patience with a dollop of half-hearted opportunism will suffice - bugger all comes to they who wait. Or to quote my favourite Chinese proverb: "A peasant must stand a long time on a hillside with his mouth wide open before a roast duck flies in."

You may mourn the death of Organization Man (sorry, Organization Person just doesn't have the same ring to it), and the predictable and secure working world he inhabited. If you are a forty-something like me, you may resent the fact that the terms of your career have been unilaterally redefined mid-stream. At whatever age you are, you may cringe at the thought of being "a brand called you" or "Chief Executive of Me plc." but the fact is that behind this clodhopping language rests the new truth about what lays ahead for all of us who need to work.

And the deal is this:

1. The Smart Career is one with design and intent: 'accidental careers' are still an option, but going with that option has never been more dangerous. So develop career purpose. People with a vision of their futures and goals linked to that vision are far more likely to succeed than those who don't. Admittedly, the world of work is changing so rapidly that there's a persuasive argument for waiting and responding. So perhaps the ideal is to have an overall sense of direction, but be ready to improvise.

2. Aim to enjoy your work: The decision for most of us is not whether to work but rather what to do. As we spend so much time at work, doesn't it make sense to try and find something we love doing?

3. Be visible: Find ways to raise your profile. Network like crazy.

4. Think ahead: Taking care of your job is not the same as taking care of your career. To avoid career inertia, schedule in regular reviews of where you and your career is heading. Consciously set out to acquire new skills and knowledge, and then start thinking about what to do when those new skills and knowledge themselves become obsolete.

5. Remember Thomas Stewart's observation that a Smart Career is one that operates in markets, not hierarchies. Take on board the words of Ralph Waldo Emerson, written in 1860, that if you want a Smart Career, "make yourself necessary to someone". Being the best little gaslamp-lighter in town is of little practical value if there are no gaslamps and no work. (". . . no gaslamps and no work" – actually, this isn't quite true. In February 2001, the GMB union demanded that a pay rise of a farthing pledged to lamplighters in 1765 should be honoured. The claim, now worth £16.32, was never settled. The union still has four members who light gas lamps outside Buckingham Palace and in the Royal Parks.)

6. Above all, trust your own judgement: By all means, take regular soundings of other people's views about where the world of work is heading but be sure to make up your own mind. A McKinsey study of AT&T in the early 1980s predicted that "the total market for mobile cellular phones will be 900,000 subscribers by the year 2000". On that original McKinsey assessment, AT&T pulled out of

the market, only to re-enter it at great expense through the purchase of McGaw in the 1990s. In these volatile times, don't rely on anybody else's view of the future.

This list, of course, is incomplete. It's a good starting place, but feel free to add another six ideas of your own.

The real point about having a Smart Career is that it involves a mixture of thinking and action. You need both – thinking without action is sterile, action without thinking lacks direction and mindfulness. You've made a good start in picking up this book (and an even better start if you've read this far!), but in itself it means little. To tweak a cliché: today is the first day of the rest of your career. So what are you going to do about it?

Annotated Bibliography

Shelves in bookshops the world over are buckling under the weight of literally thousands of books that aim to help us understand the working world and perform more effectively. Here is my personal selection of some of the most relevant and insightful.

The Dilbert Principle, Scott Adams (Boxtree, 1996)
Not since the early days of *The Far Side* by Gary Larson has there been a cartoon strip to match Dilbert, a mouthless, bespectacled computer nerd whose observations on modern business life are poignant, irreverent and painfully funny. For workers around the world, Dilbert has become an essential part of their lives, a touchstone with reality when the world around them seems to be going crazy, and a mouthpiece for their unvoiced concerns and feelings.

If you are not familiar with the work of Scott Adams, sample one of the

Dilbert anthologies (*Build a Better Life by Stealing Office Supplies* is a very good startpoint) and you will soon be smitten. If you are already familiar with Dilbert, you almost certainly have this book already.

Assertiveness at Work, Ken Back and Kate Back (McGraw-Hill, 1991)
The book sets out a number of ways in which people can handle difficult situations at work more effectively. For those who find handling awkward situations . . . well awkward, this is one of the best introductions to assertiveness techniques around. Equally, there are plenty of practical tips and suggestion for the more self-confident.

The Plain English Approach to Business Writing, Edward P. Bailey (Oxford University Press, 1997)
Written for busy professionals who want to improve the quality and clarity of their own (or their staff's) writing style, this guide is intended as an office companion. Bailey's approach is surprisingly straightforward: just write as you would talk because plain English is not only easier to read, it's also easier to write.

The Complete Guide to People Skills, Sue Bishop (Gower, 1997)
Sue Bishop's book sets out to provide a comprehensive guide to the interpersonal skills that are needed to get the best from a team. Areas covered include skills that can be applied in formal settings, such as recruitment interviews, or appraisals, as well as less formal, such as coaching or counselling; team skills to help communicate with, and develop team members; skills to handle disciplinary matters, or emotional crises, or to resolve conflict; and skills that can be used when just chatting with and enthusing individuals and the team.

Arranged alphabetically by topic, this book is very user friendly. It can be read from cover to cover or, more likely, used for reference when specific guidance is needed. At the end of each section is an exercise to help readers learn more about the skills and techniques and to apply them in their work.

Leadership and the One Minute Manager, Ken Blanchard *et al.*
(Fontana, Collins, 1987)
A highly readable introduction to the concept of Situational Leadership, a simple and practical model in which the leader demonstrates differing levels of direction and support according to the level of competence and commitment shown by the person being managed.

How to Find the Work You Love, Laurence G. Boldt (Arkana, 1996)
"The quest for the work you love – it all begins with the two simple questions: Who am I? and what in the world am I doing here?" The opening line of Boldt's book sets a tone that is far removed from the typical CV wash-'n-brushup merchants. For Boldt, doing the work you love means living your philosophy, putting your values to work and ensuring that the work you do reflects the person you really are. More a book of questions than answers, *How to Find the Work You Love* provides a thoughtful context for pondering the deeper purpose of work.

What Color is Your Parachute?, Richard Bolles (Tenspeed Press, 2000)
Probably the best-known career guidance book of all, this annually updated and revised classic from the US has been around since 1971. Originally little more than a newsletter, these days it is published in 10 languages and bought by an estimated 20,000 people a month worldwide. Despite the book's bulk, Bolles's approach boils down to three simple steps:

• Identify your talents

• Work out where you would like to apply these transferable skills

- Decide how you will pursue organizations that interest you

To guide readers through this process, *What Color is Your Parachute?* is jam-packed with useful advice and information – easy-to-read tables, charts, useful Internet site addresses, quotations and even the occasional poem. Although the book may look at first glance to be a tad new agey for some tastes, at its heart is actually a very pragmatic and proven process.

Project Leadership, 2nd edn, Briner, Hastings and Geddes (Gower, 1997)
The first edition of this book broke new ground by focusing on the leadership aspects of project management rather than the technical. In this second edition, a new section, "Preparing the Ground" reflects an increased emphasis on getting projects off to the right start, and contains some interesting insights into the scoping process designed to ensure all parties agree on objectives. It also demonstrates the importance of understanding the organizational and political factors involved if the project is to succeed in business terms. The final section contains a useful "action summary" and a guide to further resources.

Downshifting: The Ultimate Handbook, Andy Bull (Thorsons, 1998)
Billed as the "ultimate handbook" for downshifting, Andy Bull's book is really a collection of interesting and enlightening case studies of people who have made a deliberate decision to simplify their lives. As such, it could prove invaluable to anyone who is actively considering swapping a high-pressure lifestyle for a simpler, more rewarding way of life. The author offers a wealth of information derived from the real life experiences of would-be downshifters and it is a particularly interesting exercise to contrast those who have "succeeded" with those who have "failed" in their endeavours. However, it is stretching a point to call the book a comprehensive handbook. What is clearly missing is the inclu-

sion of some process materials to assist the reader in making the complex decisions that underlie a major life change.

Use Your Head, Tony Buzan (BBC Publications, 1974)
This is the book that over 25 years ago introduced Mind Maps as a tool for aiding recall and for enabling creative thinking. Buzan's ideas and general approach have not dated at all, and in Mind Mapping he has given the world arguably the most widely used creative tool of the last few decades.

Smart Things to Know about Teams, Annemarie Caracciolo
(Capstone, 1999)
Smart Things to Know about Teams is an intelligently assembled overview of the latest thinking about teams and teamworking. Annemarie Caracciolo clearly knows her topic and draws eclectically on a wide range of sources – from Senge to St Luke's and from Warren Bennis to The Bishopston Team, a team of seven women who work as community midwives. Those readers who are already steeped in the subject may find little in the book that is truly groundbreaking, but for anybody looking for a one-stop overview of the subject, *Smart Things to Know about Teams* probably can't be bettered

The Nice Factor Book, Robin Chandler and Jo Ellen Grzyb (Simon and Schuster, 1997)
Ever apologized even when you haven't done anything wrong? Do you have friends who outstay their welcome? Is it you that normally gets stuck with the party bore? Been overlooked for promotion? If you're nodding at this point, the chances are that you're too nice for your own good. Described as 'the first antidote to the national plague of overniceness', this book sets out to show you how to stand up for yourself and put your own needs first. Although much of the content of the

book is reminiscent of the sort of stuff covered on assertiveness or self-esteem workshops, the authors have in the concept of "niceness" an original and very accessible vehicle for putting over their brand of effective relationship management.

Hare Brain, Tortoise Mind, Guy Claxton (Fourth Estate, 1997)
Sometimes we think so hard that we get in our own way, argues Claxton, who believes that the human brain/mind will do a number of unusual, interesting and important things if it is given the time. It will make sense out of hazy, ill-defined situations which leave rationality flummoxed; it will get to the bottom of personal and emotional issues much more successfully than the questing intellect; and when no amount of information or computing power is ever going to be enough, Tortoise Mind will often deliver a quiet, intuitive answer, while Hare Brain is dashing frenetically and fruitlessly about. The essence of Tortoise Mind, then, is that its answers cannot be engineered, controlled or rushed in any way. Unfortunately, in a have-it-on-my-desk-by-the-morning culture, Tortoise Mind is too often starved of the gentle resources, notably time that it needs, and its abilities are neglected. *Hare Brain, Tortoise Mind* offers a fundamental challenge to the prevalent assumption that fast, purposeful thinking and more information are going to deliver answers to all our problems. It's a fascinating and important book.

Portfolio People, Max Comfort (Century Business Books, 1997)
Charles Handy is generally credited for "inventing" the idea of the work portfolio – a way of describing how the different bits of work in our life can fit together – in *The Age of Unreason*. Since that book's publication in 1989, increasing numbers of people are finding that, either through choice or necessity, they have portfolio careers. Max Comfort provides a lively and accessible guide to the subject, reporting on the personal

experiences of Portfolio People, and encouraging readers to review – through questionnaires and reflective exercises – how equipped they are to take up a portfolio career.

Executive EQ, Robert Cooper and Ayman Sawaf (Orion Business Books, 1997)
Daniel Goleman's best-selling *Emotional Intelligence*, published in 1996, claims that our emotions play a much greater role in thought, decision-making and individual success than is commonly acknowledged. *Executive EQ* (the initials stand for emotional quotient) argues that emotional intelligence will be a new driving force in business. Whether this will prove to be the case is open to question – most organizations are still not noted for their emotional maturity – but this is a self-help book with enough business examples to give the idea credibility. Readers have the opportunity to map their own emotional intelligence by completing a questionnaire at the back of the book.

The Seven Habits of Highly Effective People, Stephen R. Covey (Simon and Schuster)
This international best-seller is admired and disdained in equal measure. While critics dismiss Covey as a peddler of Californian-style psychobabble, his admirers believe that Covey offers, as the cover of his book puts it, "powerful lessons in personal change". For those not yet familiar with his work, his seven principles are:

• Be proactive

• Begin with the end in mind

• Put first things first (the principle of personal management)

• Think win–win

- Seek first to understand, then to be understood

- Synergize (the principle of creative co-operation)

- Sharpen the saw (the principle of balanced self-renewal)

If these headings strike a chord, you might find reading this book a life-changing experience. If they leave you cold, Covey is probably not for you.

Against the Odds: An Autobiography, James Dyson (Orion Business Books, 1997)
James Dyson is the inventor of the revolutionary Dual Cyclone bagless vacuum cleaner. Once rejected by the likes of Hoover and Electrolux, his machine has literally "cleaned up" and made its inventor a multimillionaire. In this book, Dyson describes his early years at the Royal College of Art, his initial successes with the Ballbarrow (a tough, stable plastic wheelbarrow with a large red plastic ball instead of a wheel), through the years spent perfecting the design of the Dual Cyclone and the battle to have it manufactured.

More autobiography than business book, there is nonetheless plenty to be gleaned here about Dyson's management methods, particularly in a chapter entitled A new philosophy of business. Much of Dyson's success, described by *The Times* as "possibly the most inspiring British business story of the late 20th century", can be attributed to the fact that he practises what most management writers preach. This, combined with his highly accessible prose style, makes his book compelling, instructive, and enjoyable to read.

The Economist Style Guide, Economist Staff (Wiley, 1998)
The Economist Style Guide is designed to promote good writing. Next

to a dictionary, this is the most thumbed reference book I have to hand when writing a letter or report (or a book, come to that).

Emotion in Organisations, Stephen Fineman (Sage, 1993)
The groundbreaking book brings together a number of contributions from leading academics about how people can behave in companies and why this should be so. Not the easiest of reads, but it does make the point powerfully that a person's behavior always appears logical to that individual, no matter how irrational it might appear to others.

Entrepreneurship and the Wired Life: Work in the Wake of Careers, Fernando Flores and John Gray (Demos, 2000)
The career, as an institution, is in unavoidable decline according to this fascinating pamphlet from independent UK think-tank Demos. The authors describe two work patterns – the Wired and the Entrepreneurial – which might supplant the traditional career. In a nutshell, the Wired pattern replaces the lifelong identity of the career with a series of "brief habits", at the heart of which is spontaneity rather than continuity of projects and relationships. With the Entrepreneurial pattern, Flores and Gray widen out the narrow economic definition of entrepreneurship to include all manner of activities which initiate meaningful change in a context of shared responsibility. This could be in commerce, service or in society in general. The authors go on to examine these new forms of working life in some detail and consider the implications for individuals and communities. They conclude that core institutions – from education to pensions – need restructuring to support these changes. At only 48 pages long, *Entrepreneurship and the Wired Life* is that rare phenomenon - a business book that could usefully have been double the length.

Leading Minds: An Anatomy of Leadership, Howard Gardner (HarperCollins, 1996)
Gardner takes a variety of well-known leaders – as diverse as Margaret Thatcher and Mahatma Gandhi – and tries to tease out what it is that made them so successful. He tops and tails his book with chapters on his theoretical framework and sandwiches the biographies in the middle. Gardner demonstrates brilliantly the qualities and experience needed by "leading minds", although less helpfully offers no practical guidance as to how readers might develop their own leadership skills.

Managing Your Time, Sally Garratt (Fontana, 1985)
Aimed at those for whom the working day isn't long enough to fit everything in, this book is short, practical, realistic and full of real-life examples. Readers are encouraged to complete a time management questionnaire and to maintain a time log as ways of gaining insight into how they manage their time. The centrepiece of the book consists of three sections on "How to Organise Yourself", "How to Manage Your Team" and "How to Organise Your Office". There is also a section on how to read and write more effectively.

The E-myth Revisited, Michael Gerber (Harper Business, 1995)
The "e-" in this case stands for "entrepreneurial" rather than the more fashionable "electronic". Gerber explores why most small businesses don't work and what can be done about it. He makes the vital distinction between working on your business and working in your business, in other words between managing a business and being a business.

Getting a Life, Polly Ghazi and Judy Jones (Hodder & Stoughton, 1997)
In *Getting a Life*, Ghazi and Jones provide a good insight into the downshifting movement. In the first half of the book they deal with

conceptual matters; the roots of movement in the US, the marked changes in employment and employability over the last decade and the current British experience with downshifting. In the second half they turn to the practical matters of how to downshift. Here they cover not only the financial essentials but also a broad array of topics including health, feng shui, and our contribution to community. If you are one of those people who refuse to see the world in terms of black or white but prefer shades of grey, this book is for you. The world, it turns out, is not composed of "downshifters" and conventional employees. We are not forced to choose between the two. It is, rather, a question of which elements of the downshifting movement we might like to incorporate into our lives.

My Brilliant Career, Jeff Grout and Lynne Curry (Kogan Page, 2000)
In which some of the UK's best-known rich and famous personalities from the media, business and sporting worlds divulge what they believe to be the secrets of their extraordinary success. People like Sebastian Coe, Raymond Blanc, Sir Chay Blythe, Harvey Goldsmith, Nicola Horlick, Michael Parkinson, Tony Robinson and cricket's Robin Smith reveal what got them to the top, whether they would do it again, or whether they have any regrets.

The Hungry Spirit, Charles Handy (Hutchinson, 1997)
The hungry spirit sees Handy drawing together his business and spiritual interests as he looks at how the rawer aspects of capitalism can co-exist with the search for an inner meaning to life. Different readers will form different conclusions about *The Hungry Spirit*. Those who share Handy's quest for meaning in work and life will find much to applaud; more pragmatic readers in search of new business ideas will feel partially stimulated but ultimately short-changed.

The New Alchemists, Charles Handy (Hutchinson, 1999)

At the heart of *The New Alchemists* is a series of interviews with 29 people who have made something out of nothing in either the business or arts worlds, or for the community. Those featured include inventor Trevor Baylis (creator of the clockwork radio), Andy Law of the St Luke's ad agency, Geoff Mulgan (founder of Demos), Tim Waterstone of the eponymous bookshop, BA's Bob Ayling (whose inclusion seems open to question, to be honest) and the UK's Master Alchemist Richard Branson. And what makes an Alchemist? According to Handy, they have three over-riding qualities:

- Dedication: caring passionately about what they are trying to bring into being.

- Doggedness: a wholehearted commitment to achieving results through hard work, determination and tenacity.

- Difference: a mixture of personality and talent that leads Alchemists to do things differently or to do different things

At one level, *The New Alchemists* would grace any managerial bookshelf – it is beautifully designed and it takes on a genuinely interesting topic. However, I can't help feeling that Handy has produced one of the first business coffee-table books when he should have been using the same material to write the *Harvard Business Review* article of the year.

Proven Management Models, Sue Harding and Trevor Long (Gower, 1998)

This book usefully brings together 45 of the key models used in management diagnosis and problem solving. They cover the areas of strategy, organization, human resources and marketing, and feature a mixture of the familiar and the less well known. For each model, the authors provide: a diagrammatic representation of the model; the principle of which the model is based; the underlying assumptions; the issues involved; guidance on using the model; related models; and further reading about the model.

As a single source book covering the likes of Belbin's team types, Maslow's hierarchy of needs, SWOT analysis, the Seven S model, Ansoff's box, the BCG matrix, Porter's five forces, the Geobusiness model, Cultural Webs, Pestlied and so on, this is a very useful reference work to have on the bookshelves. Although there is nothing new in this book – the emphasis being very much on tried and tested models – *Proven Management Models* could save you hours of fruitless searching for that dimly recalled photocopy of a model that you're sure resides somewhere in the filing system.

Be Your Own Life Coach, Fiona Harrold (Hodder & Stoughton, 2000)
With an emphasis on the practical, and making extensive use of case studies as well as affirmations and motivational techniques, *Be Your Own Life Coach* sets out ten steps to help people take control of their lives. Underpinning the book is Harrold's evident conviction that "when you believe in yourself, anything is possible", in other words, that deeply ingrained beliefs and behavior can be changed by sheer force of will. She takes the reader through a number of exercises that examine two building blocks of confidence – self-belief and personal power. Harrold is a powerful and persuasive writer and it is clear that many readers respond to her unfaltering faith in her own worldview. Those looking for more shades of grey should probably go elsewhere for their inspiration.

301 Ways to Have Fun at Work, Dave Hemsath and Leslie Yerkes
(Berrett Koehler, 1997)
Acts of fun, say Hemsath and Yerkes, "increase productivity and morale
and have a positive effect on the bottom line." Some of their suggestions
– begin meetings with foam dart fights, hold relay races in office chairs,
keep a toy box in every conference room, and deliver messages by
attaching them to Frisbees, etc. – are probably too outlandish to catch
on in the UK. Others are faintly sinister (set up a Fun Project Team
whose mission is to identify opportunities for organizational mirth).
However, the intention behind the book, namely to encourage organizations to use humour as a means of humanizing the workplace, is
laudable and some of the suggestions do seem like, well, fun.

The Excellent Manager's Companion, Philip Holden (Gower, 1998)
There is a growing publishing phenomenon that is aimed at providing
the business reader with "everything you want to know about management but don't have the time to read a whole book about". *The
Excellent Manager's Companion* is one of the better examples of the
genre, containing as it does 21 chapters of around ten pages each on
topics like corporate culture, customer orientation, empowerment, total
quality, leadership, career planning, and time management.

Starting and Running a Business on the Internet, Tim Ireland (Take
That Ltd, 2000)
Coming in at just 109 pages, *Starting and Running a Business on the
Internet* is an admirably concise and accessible guide for those wanting
to know the practical steps involved in setting up a successful Internet
business, from first conception through to promoting the site. A cau-
tionary note, though. Ireland's particular strength rests in his
knowledge of the mechanics of setting up a new Internet business –
from acquiring a domain name, through to 'going live' and taking

orders from around the world. He does not does not set out a provide a fully comprehensive guide to the overall business start-up process and so readers will find nothing on raising capital, hiring staff, business planning and so on. These reservations aside, this book is a useful *vade mecum* for anybody brave enough to seek the mantle of Internet entrepreneur.

Simplicity, Bill Jensen (HarperCollins, 2000)
One of the few books written from the knowledge worker's perspective. Jam-packed with tools and techniques for the individual, but also contains some useful insights on to how to build corporate infrastructures so the company is the tool of the worker, not the other way around. Also worth checking out www.simplerwork.com, the companion website.

The Wisdom of Teams, Jon Katzenbach and Douglas Smith (Harvard Business School Press, 1993)
According to Katzenbach and Smith – two senior McKinsey consultants – teams are "the primary building blocks of company performance". For this book, the authors talked with hundreds of people in more than 50 teams from 30 companies in a bid to discover what differentiates various levels of team performance, where and how teams work best, and how generally to enhance team effectiveness. Some of their findings are common sense – e.g. teams with a genuine commitment to performance goals and to a common purpose outperform those who place a greater emphasis on team-building. Others are at face value surprising (formal hierarchy, they say, is actually good for teams). In a chapter towards the end of the book they describe how top management can usefully support the development of a team-based culture.

Kennedy on Negotiation, Gavin Kennedy (Gower, 1998)
Gavin Kennedy is an authoritative and respected writer and consultant on the negotiation process. This highly practical book uses his well-established "Four Phases" model to pull together his thinking about optimal approaches to negotiating. The four phases are:-

- Prepare: What do we want?

- Debate: What do they want?

- Propose: What "wants" might we trade?

- Bargain: What "wants" will we trade?

Kennedy goes into the each phase in detail, offering a mix of wise insight and practical tips. He also constructively critiques a number of competing negotiating theories and models.

The 80/20 Principle, Richard Koch (Nicholas Brealey, 1997)
Richard Koch has taken the so-called Pareto effect – that 80% of results flow from just 20% of the causes – and applied it to individuals, organizations and society at large. His research into business, for example, shows that it is not unusual for 20% of products to generate 80% of sales, or for 20% of customers to account for 80% of a company's business. Koch suggests that individuals and groups can achieve much more with much less effort, and sets out a number of strategies for doing this. *The 80/20 Principle* is an unusual and generally convincing combination of legitimate business analysis tool and a life-changing self-help method. The book itself is easy to read and full of provocative ideas.

Open Minds, Andy Law (Orion, 1998)
Andy Law was the driving force behind the setting up of London-based

advertising agency St Luke's and has been the company's iconoclastic chairman since 1995.

St Luke's is owned entirely by its employees. All physical resources – offices, desks, PCs, etc. – are shared, there is little hierarchy, and all employees are involved in almost all decisions, including setting their own pay rises. Rose the cleaner, one of 100 employees at the company, receives the same number of shares every year as Law himself.

In the book, Law comes over as part Tom Peters, part David Icke, but with an endearing habit of not taking himself too seriously (in a recent interview with the *Financial Times*, he declared: "Half of what I say is shit").

Whether the model developed at St Luke's has the resilience to cope with a downturn in its business fortunes (the company has enjoyed continuous growth since its creation) or any future departure of Andy Law remains to be seen. In the meantime, *Open Minds* makes a compelling case study, describing and explaining as it does the business practices and philosophy behind this fascinating company.

Living on Thin Air, Charles Leadbeater (Viking, 1999)
What do you make to earn your living? Do you make anything tangible that can be weighed, measured or touched? For most people, says Leadbeater, the answer to the second question is no, with more and more of us making our living from thin air – from our ideas and our know-how. In *Living on Thin Air*, Leadbeater explores the societal implications of this phenomenon, coming as it does at a time of increasing economic and job insecurity. He argues that society will need to be organized around the creation of knowledge capital and social capital, rather than simply being dominated by the power of financial capital. He puts over

his ideas in a highly informative and accessible way and argues his case well, although some readers may feel that his take on the future is a tad more optimistic than the facts seem to justify.

Why Flip a Coin?, H.W. Lewis (Wiley, 1997)
It is rare to come across a book that can truly be called fascinating, but here is one. *Why Flip a Coin?* is about the science of making decisions of all kinds – from choosing whom to marry to gambling on the Stock Exchange – with such things as probability theory, puzzles and random walks thrown in. *Why Flip a Coin?* is practical, enlightening, witty and sometimes hilarious. At the end of it, you will be far better equipped to deal with the thousands of decisions you have to make during your life, and have had a whale of a time.

The Pathfinder: How to Choose or Change Your Career for a Lifetime of Satisfaction and Success, Nicholas Lore (Simon & Schuster, 1998)
For those interested in questions of "meaning, mission and purpose", this book comes with over one hundred self-tests and exercises designed to help you make explicit your natural aptitudes, interests, and values.

40 Checklists for Managers and Team Leaders, Ian MacKay (Gower, 1993)
Recently republished, the late Ian MacKay's book does not, as the title of the book might suggest, provide a set of easy answers for managers simply to apply. Rather he offers a collection of useful prompts and questions designed to help them tackle problems in a structured way. The book focuses on some of the most common areas of managerial concern – coaching, delegation, interviewing, making a presentation and so on.

Stress and Relaxation, Jane Madders (Optima, 1979)
Jane Madders taught stress management techniques for over 40 years. Her book is a thorough and informed guide to the numerous relaxation techniques available. There are more chatty, user-friendly books around on the subject but this book is ideal for those seeking sensible, unfussy advice.

The Pyramid Principle, Barbara Minto (Pitman, 1991)
Based on the concept that any grouping of ideas is easier to comprehend if it is pre-sorted into a logical structure, *The Pyramid Principle* looks at the use of logic in thinking and writing. Minto sets out a number of techniques aimed at helping people to analyse complex information and then provides a comprehensive structure for setting out information clearly and logically. She goes on to show how using her methods can enable complex subjects to be clearly and quickly understood when presented in writing or face-to-face. For my money, this is an indispensable writing manual – the best around on how good writing flows from clear thinking

The Innovator's Handbook, Vincent Nolan (Sphere, 1987)
A very readable and highly practical guide to original ideas – how to get them, how to put them into action, and how to create the right work environment for them.

Simply Speaking: How to Communicate Your Ideas with Style,
Substance and Clarity, Peggy Noonan (Harper Audio, 1998)
Peggy Noonan achieved fame as chief political scriptwriter for two American presidents – Ronald Reagan and George Bush. On this tape, she shares her secrets for effective oral communication, speaking with clarity, warmth and ease throughout. Although some may find the tape a

bit too folksy and, well, American, many people will find something of value in her simple but effective balance of logic and heart.

The "How To" Guide for Managers, John and Shirley Payne (Gower, 1996)
A determinedly practical book that contains 110 ideas grouped under 11 key skills of management, including objective setting, delegation, time management, communication, making decisions, and running meetings. There is little here that is truly new or original but that is probably not the point. More significantly, perhaps, a senior manager friend borrowed the book and pronounced it "very useful".

The Brand New You: Reinventing Work, Tom Peters (Knopf, 1999)
With the publication of *In Search of Excellence* in 1982, Tom Peters and co-author Bob Waterman changed the way organizations thought about themselves. Notions of embracing a paradoxical world of constant change, of providing exemplary customer service and of the need for high-speed response are now mainstream corporate thinking, but during the mid-1980s, when he was at the peak of his fame, the challenge laid down by Peters was enormous. In recent years, Peters has focused increasingly on how changes at a corporate, national and global level impact on the nature of work for us as individuals, and in August 1997, he contributed an article to *Fast Company* magazine called "The Brand Called You: You Can't Move Up if You Don't Stand Out". It's a brilliant synthesis of economic, marketing and business themes that ends with a stark conclusion: "It's this simple: you are a brand. You are in charge of your brand. There is no single path to success. And there is no one right way to create the brand called You. Except this: Start today. Or else."

Two years later Peters expanded the article into book form with *Brand You 50*. Underpinning the book is Peters' passionate belief that the individual has become the fundamental unit in the new economy. The book consists of, in his words, "fifty ways to transform yourself from an employee into a brand that shouts distinction, commitment and passion".

Reality Hacking, Nicola Phillips (Capstone, 1997)
It's an indication of this book's general approach that readers are invited to start and finish reading it anywhere they like. Using a mixture of provocative questions and inspirational quotes, and working from the principle that "the best way to enjoy your future is to invent it yourself", Phillips encourages the reader to reconsider their assumptions about their work and their life. Some will find this book inspirational and life-changing, others will dismiss it as pretentious psychobabble. It is a paradox that Phillips would relish that both groups may well have a point.

The Drama of Leadership, Patricia Pitcher (John Wiley, 1997)
This book is the product of an eight-year study of leadership by Canadian Professor Patricia Pitcher. She identifies three types of leaders:

- Artists, who are people-oriented, open-minded, intuitive and visionary;

- Craftsmen, humane, dedicated, often conservative people who take pride in a job well done, and who are committed to quality workmanship;

- Technocrats, well schooled in theory, detail-oriented, methodical, and self-centred.

Each type of leader comes to the fore in different circumstances (Artists when the need is for a new vision, Craftsmen when a company has to get back to basics and re-establish a commitment to quality, and Technocrats to chop and hack a way to survival). According to Pitcher, Technocrat leaders have dominated organizations in recent years. She would like to see more Craftsmen leading organizations as they would give Artists room to breathe and time to create, and they could keep Technocrats in their legitimate place.

Exploding a number of popular myths about leaders on the way, *The Drama of Leadership* is an insightful and passionate appeal to rethink the type of people that organizations will need at the helm in the 21st century. Relatively light on practical guidance though

Competitive Strategy, Michael Porter (Free Press, 1980)
What forces drive competition in an industry? How can a company be best placed to compete in the long run? Porter's book, radical in its day, was one of the first to look the whole field of competitive strategy. His work has entered the management mainstream and his techniques for analysing industries and competitors are now widely used. For anybody wishing to increase their awareness of the industry or competitive context that they work in, Porter's models and techniques remain valid and easy to use.

The Internet Start-Up Bible, Tess Read, Callum Chace and Simon Rowe (Random House, 2000)
The Internet Start-Up Bible is an accessible, well-written guide about how to plan, research, fund, market and implement a successful Internet-based business model. The authors take the logical and too often neglected step of applying the same success criteria to dot.com business start-ups as to traditional ventures. Important sections on the entrepreneurial mindset, the process of shaping ideas into marketable concepts and employing and managing people are included. Detailed chapters on business planning and attracting venture capital are fol-

lowed by sections on various aspects of starting up an Internet business; technology, design, marketing and launch, before concluding with business growth and flotation. The book is crammed with useful case studies, extensive links and contact addresses and running quotes from business gurus and key books.

Scenario Planning, Gill Ringland (Wiley, 1998)
Gill Ringland, ICL's Group Executive with responsibility for strategy at the time of writing, adds her contribution to the recent flurry of books published about scenario planning. Unlike other books on the subject, this is written by a dry-eyed general management practitioner rather than a business school academic, and gives a good insight into the mechanics of scenario planning and the practical benefits that the approach can offer.

Those with greater familiarity with the subject will get more from either *Scenarios: The Art of Strategic Conversation* by Kees van der Heijden (Wiley, 1996) or *The Art of the Long View* by Peter Schwartz (Wiley, 1991).

Soloing: Reaching Life's Everest, Harriet Rubin (Random House, 1999)
Few of us can aspire to the heights of the people Rubin quotes, who retreat to stunning locations to think and turn down all but the most fascinating jobs. That said, it's hard not to like this book. It is crammed with practical ideas, unconventional wisdom and handy hints. And, apart from the worst cynics among us, who can resist anyone who insists that we must learn our livings? Maybe Rubin is right. Perhaps we can all arrive at the point where we, "get so good at doing only what [we] love that work feels like play".

Gower Handbook of Management Skills, ed. Dorothy M. Stewart (Gower, 1998)
The third edition of this best-selling handbook is the sort of book that we could all have done with when we first became managers. Divided into three parts – "Managing Yourself", "Managing Other People" and "Managing Business" – it is crammed full of sound guidance and advice from a host of recognized authorities in their fields. Part 1 deals with personal skills and includes chapters on self-development and IT. Part 2 covers people skills, such as listening, influencing and communication. Part 3 looks at finance, project management, decision-making, negotiating and creativity. Each chapter ends with a checklist of key points and suggestions for further reading. *The Gower Handbook of Management Skills* exudes plain-speaking common sense throughout its 430 pages and is ideal for new or aspiring managers seeking a one-stop reference book.

Rapid Problem-solving with Post-It® Notes, David Straker (Gower, 1997)
Like many of the best ideas, using Post-It® notes as a medium for problem-solving seems an obvious application now that David Straker has written this excellent book. The book is in three sections, the first a general introduction to the nature of problems and problem-solving, the second a description of six problem-solving techniques that make use of Post-It® notes, and the final section provides a problem-solving framework plus tips on how to make the tools work to best effect. Full of worked examples, illustrations and regular summaries, this is a highly practical and accessible book.

Do What You Are, Paul D. Tieger and Barbara Barron-Tieger (Little Brown, 1995)
Subtitled "Discover the Perfect Career for You Through the Secrets of

Personality", this book uses the Myers–Briggs Type Indicator (if you haven't come across MBTI, it's a brilliant psychometric questionnaire derived from the work of Carl Jung) to help readers identify careers suited to their personal strengths. *Do What You Are* explains why personality type is so important in a job search, but also lets you figure out your own type, and find your perfect slot in the job world.

For a general introduction to MBTI itself, try *Please Understand Me* by David Keirsey and Marilyn Bates (Prometheus Nemesis, 1978).

Liberating Leadership, David Turner (The Industrial Society, 1998)
Based on the results of extensive survey research conducted by the Industrial Society into what people really value in their leaders, *Liberating Leadership* is jam-packed with checklists, real-life company examples and anecdotes which describe what David Turner calls a new style of leadership that is needed in today's organizations. He uses the mnemonic LEADER to illustrate the key beliefs and behaviours of the liberating leader:

- L   Liberates

- E   Encourages and supports

- A   Achieves purpose

- D   Develops people and teams

- E   Example setting

- R   Relationship-building through trust

Clearly laid out and pleasingly concise at around 150 pages, *Liberating Leadership* is a highly readable book that offers practical guidance, which is grounded in real-life case studies, and which is backed up by solid research.

A Whack on the Side of the Head, Roger von Oech (Thorsons, 1983)
According to Roger von Oech, the secret of being more creative is to be able to look at the world in a different way. This book is well illustrated, and filled with puzzles, anecdotes, exercises, cartoons, quotations, questions, stories and tips designed to "whack" the reader out of their traditional thought patterns and into new, creative ways of thinking.

Managers as Facilitators, Richard Weaver and John Farrell (Berrett Koehler, 1997)
According to Weaver and Farrell, successful managers must use facilitation skills to help people exercise the freedom to make decisions, respond quickly to customers, work together more effectively, and produce the results needed by their organizations. They say that to become a successful facilitator, one must recognize and use the four key elements of the facilitation model: task, self, group and process. They explore each element in detail, and offer step-by-step guidance to applying the model to real work situations.

Managers as Facilitators is an excellent source of ideas to use as a team develops and changes. The chapter on change will give many readers insightful "ahas" of recognition as they reflect on organisational changes they have experienced. Real-world examples make the book accessible as well as practical, and a Quick Fix section offers excellent clues to solving everyday management problems.

The Lloyds TSB Small Business Guide, Sara Williams (Penguin, updated annually)
For a jargon-free, yet thorough guide to what's involved in setting yourself up in business, you probably can't do better than this.

Smart Sources

Internet Sites

There's a lot of career-related sites out there. The following are some of the best I've come across. If you have any suggestions for inclusion, please let me know.

Big Small Business Initiative: **www.bsbi.co.uk**
Good source of information on some of the basics like accounting and technology.

British Library: **www.bl.uk/collections/newspaper/sources.html**
The British Library holds a good listing of online newspapers, divided into the following categories: London, Scottish, Irish, English and Welsh, Channel Islands and Isle of Man, and Newspapers around the world. A helpful resource if you are planning to move to another area.

British Venture Capital Association: **www.bvca.co.uk**
A useful source to check out if you are seeking funding to launch or grow a business.

BT directory enquiries: **www.bt.co.uk/phonenetuk/**
For anyone that might need it, BT directory enquiries are online and free of charge

Business 2.0: **www.business2.com**
Recently launched in the UK by Future Publishing, *Business 2.0* is a monthly magazine that is jam-packed with intelligent and insightful articles on the New Economy. If it maintains the promise and high content level of its early issues, it could rapidly become a first port of call for anybody wanting to track where the dot-com world might be heading.

Business Intelligence: **www.business-intelligence.co.uk/**
Publisher of some solid but very expensive reports (typically around £600 a copy). Website carries some useful free material though.

Centre for Business Innovation: **www.businessinnovation.ey.com**
Site managed by consultants Ernst and Young – quality of content varies but occasionally provokes thought.

Charities

www.charity-executives.co.uk
The site for Charity and Fundraising Appointments (CF Appointments Ltd).

www.charitychoice.co.uk
This website is a good starting point if you want to find out about a particular charity. There is a category search page, which gives you a choice of topics (hospices, blind, etc.), and when you click on to a topic it brings up a list of the relevant charities.

www.volwork.org.uk
If you do wish to do some voluntary work, this site will help you find a role suitable to your skills.

www.charity-commission.gov.uk
The Charity Commission's website lists all the registered charities in the UK with information on what they do and an official point of contact.

Company information

www.carol.co.uk
A useful port of call for anyone researching a company. Although aimed main at potential investors, it is a free corporate on-line service offering one-stop access to annual reports, and providing direct links to over 3,000 corporate reports in a single and consistent format.

Also worth checking out is **www.hemscott.co.uk** for profiles of companies, lots of data, and the facility to order free annual reports from site.

Companies House: **www.companieshouse.co.uk**
A good resource to check out if you are considering setting up a limited company. Plenty of information as well as downloadable copies of the relevant forms.

DTI Enterprise Zone: **www.enterprisezone.org.uk**
DTI Enterprise Zone provides business information and access to finance legal and technical data for small firms. Launched by DTI using information from Business Links.

The Economist: **www.economist.com**

The best single source of information about what is happening in the world. A mainstream publication but one that will take on some big topics from time to time, and one whose take on the new economy is variably insightful and clear-eyed.

Executive Grapevine: **www.d-net.com/executive.grapevine_**

Fast Company: **www.fastcompany.com/home.html**
The magazine is monthly and has been an essential read since it started up in 1996. Of late, though, the content – while still excellent – has been swamped by increasing volumes of advertising. That said, the companion website is just about the best free site around on the increasing number of people who have flown the corporate nest and set up on their own. It also carries material not found in the magazine.

Financial Times: **www.ft.com** and **www.ft.com/connectis**
Of all the dailies, *The Financial Times* provides the best in-depth coverage of work-related issues. Andy Hobsbawm's column – @ The Chat Room – in the Saturday *FT* is invariably thought provoking and topical about the various ways in which technology is impacting on our lives. Also well worth keeping an eye out for their occasional information technology surveys as well as their monthly e-business magazine *Connectis*.

Fish4jobs: **www.fish4jobs.co.uk**
A database that is improving month by month – worth using if looking for a local job.

Fucked Company: **www.fuckedcompany.com**
An irreverent spoof of Fast Company that, like the very best Dilbert car-

toons, uses humour as a vehicle for revealing some painful truths about working life.

Guardian: **www.jobsunlimited.co.uk**
The *Guardian*'s jobs website. The *Guardian* covers a wide spread of vacancies, but is particularly strong on media, public sector and charity roles.

Harvard Business Review: **www.hbsp.harvard.edu/home.html**
The most authoritative business monthly on the block. Has tended in the past to be more mainstream than truly groundbreaking in its coverage of business issues. That said, recent issues have generally contained two or three good articles. Also, if you are interested in getting the lowdown on forthcoming books from Harvard's publishing wing several months before publication, the magazine consistently trails major books with articles from the authors. The website provides overview of contents of the magazine – no free articles but the executive summaries are there and they are often all you need.

Information Economy: **www.sims.berkeley.edu/resources/infoecon/**
This website is overseen by economist Hal Varian, co-author of *Information Rules*, and lists hundreds of papers, works in progress, and links to other new economy websites. An almost overwhelming resource but one that hasn't been bettered.

Information Society Initiative: **www.isi.gov.uk**
Sponsored by the UK government's Department of Trade and Industry, the Information Society Initiative is intended to encourage businesses to get involved in e-commerce. The website contains informative material including some particularly useful (and free) CD-ROMs on the subject of doing business electronically.

Inland Revenue: **www.inlandrevenue.gov.uk**
A comprehensive site that combines copious information on just about
every aspect of employment and self-employment plus lots of downloadable files.

Interim Management Association: **www.interimmanagement.uk.com**
Previously known as ATIES (the Association of Temporary and Interim
Executive Services), the Interim Management Association was launched
in the spring of 2001. Their site contains a directory of members (with
website links) as well as their code of practise.

Interim Management: **www.fres.co.uk_**
Another good source of information on interim management.

International Association of Career Management Professionals:
www.iacmp.org
Some useful information about the latest career management practices.

Internet Business:
Just about the best of the recent flurry of new monthlies about the doing
business on the internet. Informative mix of case studies, interviews,
book extracts and topical news stories.

Management Link: **www.inst.mgt.org.uk/external/mgt-link**
A one-stop shop containing links to more than 100 key management
websites.

Ministry of Silly regulations: **www.sillyregs.co.uk**
An excellent website for small businesses featuring details of regulations
affecting areas like agriculture, small business, employment and tax.

The Monster Board: **www.monster.co.uk**
Job opportunities in the UK, the US and elsewhere. There is a facility for applying on-line.

New Scientist: **www.newscientist.com**
Important science and technology stories will often appear here first. *New Scientist* also gives good coverage to emerging thinking in the scientific community.

New Thinking: **http://list.adventive.com/SCRIPTS/WA.EXE?SUBED1 =new-thinking&A=1**
New Thinking is a weekly, approximately 500-word exploration of the digital age, produced by Gerry McGovern, CEO of Nua and author of *The Caring Economy*. Taking a broad, philosophical view of things, it is written in clear, concise language and delivers some useful comments and ideas. It is available by email and is free. To subscribe to New Thinking either: send a blank email to: mailto: new-thinking-join-request@list.adventive.com; or go to the website.

People Management: **www.peoplemanagement.co.uk**
The online magazine of the Chartered Institute of Personnel and Development

Press Association: **www.ananova.com/**
This is the Press Association's website, which has a useful search engine.

Recruitment and Employment Confederation: **www.rec.uk.com**
The industry's association web site. Contains details of the members' codes of practise, and if you wish to complain about a recruiter, this is a good place to start.

Red Herring: **www.redherringcom**
A monthly magazine that looks at the companies and trends that are shaping the business of technology. Although occasionally prone to obsess about the technology itself rather than the impact of the technology, *Red Herring* is nonetheless a worthwhile investment for the generalist reader.

Revolution: **www.revolution.haynet.com/**
UK-published weekly about business and marketing in the digital economy. More "newsy" than considered and analytical, it's nonetheless a good read and gives better coverage than any other daily or weekly.

Start Up Failures: **www.startupfailures.com**
A website that offers support to people who have joined the dot-com mania and failed. Although the site has been known to sell T-shirts bearing the motto "If disco can make a comeback, so can you", the overall intent is serious – visitors are offered the opportunity to share dot-com experiences and access to job listings for those keen to try again.

Daily Telegraph: **www.telegraph.co.uk**
A useful website to check out their job advertisements.

Think Tanks: **www.demos.co.uk/linkuk.htm**
Good startpoint for exploring all the UK's major think-tanks

The Utne Reader: **www.utne.com**
A digest, whose editors scan thousands of small and alternative magazines. Not that well focused perhaps, but worth visiting for occasional gems.

Time: **www.time.com/europe**

Weekly news magazine that gives good, positive coverage to the latest work issues. That said, *Time* is a mainstream publication and so is unlikely to be absolutely at the forefront of business thinking. Nonetheless, it does from time to time carry special features on e-commerce, the future of work, and so on.

The Times: **www.the-times.co.uk** and **www.sunday-times.co.uk**

Total Jobs: **www.totaljobs.com**
Online jobs services from Reed International. It has all the advertisements from Reed International Publications (*New Scientist*, *Computer Weekly*, etc.) Very professional site.

Washington Post: **www.washingtonpost.com/parachute**
Surprisingly good source of information about online job-hunting and career changing resources.

Wired: **www.wired.com/wired/**
Monthly American magazine that is good at picking up technology-based trends about six months before they become trends.

www.aboutwork.com
Chat room and discussion group where participants explore all aspects of the world of work. More interesting than it sounds.

www.americasemployers.com
America's employers – on-line career services to connect job seekers with employers.

www.agencycentral.co.uk
This site compiles tables of links to job sites by industry sector.

www.agenciesdirect.com
Site with global reach. You register, place your CV with them, and they then contact agencies in the countries you wish to go to.

www.alljobsuk.com
You can use this site to search for an agency that covers your area of work, with links to their website if they have one. You can also search for job sites, and you can also look for regional press and trade journals on line.

www.careercity.com
US site that contains interesting articles and snippets such as tips for interviews, covering letters, dress, job search.

www.careermag.com
Career magazine website with jobs, employer profiles, directories of recruiters, job fair listings and a CV bank.

www.careersinrecruitment.com
A site purely for the recruitment industry that offers jobs, news and advice.

www.careermapper.com
Offers some useful self-administered career assessment.

www.ecominfocenter.com
Good all round US e-commerce site full of good marketing tips plus some worthwhile links.

www.e-comm.webopedia.com
Good startpoint for anybody baffled by the terms used in e-business.

www.firstdivisionjobs.co.uk
Features positions from the administrative and secretarial world.

www.flexecutive.co.uk
A recruitment service that will match executives into job shares. It also sets out the special qualities needed to ensure successful job sharing.

www.graduatebase.com
Specifically for graduates, a good recruitment and information site.

www.homerun.co.uk
Site for homeworkers and small businesses.

www.i-resign.com
Contains some spectacularly silly resignation letters.

www.jobpilot.co.uk
A British Airways-sponsored site with more than 50,000 job categories. You can post your CV into the site's database and also get your own mailbox into which employers can send job-details via e-mail.

www.jobs.ac.uk
Excellent site for jobs in the academic sector.

www.jobsathome.co.uk
Winner of a competition staged to find the 'Start-up Star' of 2001, this website is designed to form an exchange for people who want to find work that can be done at home.

www.tft.co.uk
Technologies for Training – DfEE backed national consortium – the

website provides an information and advisory service for those keen to use information technology.

www.topjobs.co.uk
A number of blue-chip international companies – Sony, Cadbury Schweppes, Procter & Gamble, Standard Life, etc. – post jobs on this site.

www.workingsolo.com
Publications, audio and video products aimed at people who are interested at working on their own.

Index